OSPREY COMBAT AIRCRAFT • 6

JUNKERS Ju 87
IN NORTH AFRICA AND
THE MEDITERRANEAN

SERIES EDITOR: TONY HOLMES

OSPREY COMBAT AIRCRAFT · 6

JUNKERS Ju 87
IN NORTH AFRICA AND THE MEDITERRANEAN

John Weal

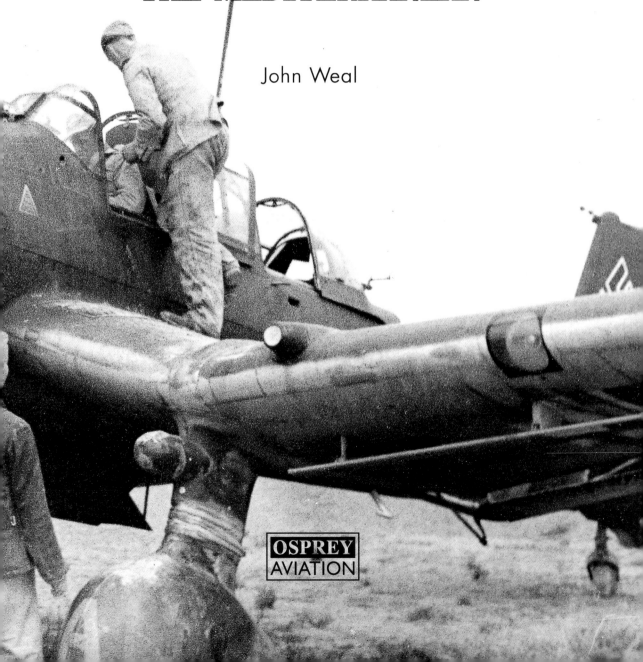

OSPREY
AVIATION

Front cover
A Ju 87R trop of 6./StG 2, based at nearby Tmimi (this airfield was used for many of the shuttle-bombing raids flown against Allied targets along the eastern Libyan coast in 1941-42), dives down on the beleaguered port town of Tobruk in mid-1941. This garishly-marked Stuka was the regular mount of Leutnant Hubert Pölz, who later won a Knight's Cross and Oak Leaves on the Eastern Front. He finished the war as *Kommandeur* of I./SG 151
(*Cover painting by Iain Wyllie*)

First published in Great Britain in 1998 by Osprey Publishing
Michelin House, 81 Fulham Road, London SW3 6RB

ISBN 1 85532 722 8

Edited by Tony Holmes
Page design by TT Designs, T & S Truscott
Cover Artwork by Iain Wyllie
Aircraft Profiles by John Weal
Figure Artwork by Mike Chappell
Scale Drawings by Mark Styling

Printed in Hong Kong

ACKNOWLEDGEMENTS
Both the author and the editor would like to thank Philip Jarrett, Herrn Generalleutnant aD. Helmut Mahlke, Holger Nauroth, Dr Alfred Price, Georg Schlaug, Robert Simpson, Ulrich Weber, *Aeroplane* and Aerospace Publishing for the provision of photographs for inclusion in this volume – a belated thank you also to the late Heinz J Nowarra and Janusz Piekalkiewicz for supplying material a number of years ago. Finally, the author acknowledges that some of the Stuka crewmembers' accounts quoted in these pages come from translations made by him from contemporary German records held in his collection.

EDITOR'S NOTE
To make this best-selling series as authoritative as possible, the editor would be extremely interested in hearing from any individual who may have relevant photographs, documentation or first-hand experiences relating to the elite pilots, and their aircraft, of the various theatres of war. Any material used will be fully credited to its original source. Please write to Tony Holmes at 10 Prospect Road, Sevenoaks, Kent, TN13 3UA, Great Britain.

CONTENTS

FROM THE ENGLISH CHANNEL TO THE SICILIAN NARROWS

For the first year of the war the Junkers Ju 87 dive-bomber had enjoyed a fearsome reputation. In conjunction with the Panzer divisions on the ground, it formed the very core of the *Blitzkrieg* concept, spearheading the Wehrmacht's rampaging drives through Poland, the Low Countries and France. The unmistakable crank-winged silhouette of approaching Ju 87s – the banshee wail as they tipped over into their near vertical dives directly overhead – was enough to unnerve all but the most disciplined of troops. The mere mention of the word 'Stuka' could spread panic among the columns of civilian refugees thronging the roads of Belgium and France in the early summer of 1940.

It was not until Reichsmarschall Göring ordered his Ju 87 *Gruppen* across the Channel to attack targets in southern England in August of that year that the Stukas' seemingly unstoppable progress was brought to a halt with all the suddenness and finality of a car slamming into a brick wall. The myth was shattered. The Luftwaffe's planners had to face an unpalatable truth – in hostile airspace, against determined and organised fighter opposition, the Ju 87 was fatally vulnerable. Never again would serried formations of Stukas prowl at will in the daylight skies of north-west Europe (see companion volume *Osprey Combat Aircraft 1 - Ju 87 Stukageschwader 1937-41* for further details).

There was, however, another theatre of war where the enemy's (pre-dominantly obsolescent) fighter strength was not only spread much more thinly, but also completely devoid of the sophisticated early-warning radar and ground-control organisations which had proved so decisive during the Battle of Britain. When, therefore, on 10 December 1940 Hitler sanctioned the transfer of the anti-shipping X.*Fliegerkorps* from Norway down to Sicily to assist his southern ally Mussolini in the Mediterranean, the opportunity was taken to add to this force two of the semi-redundant *Stukagruppen* which had lain idle in the Pas de Calais since the cross-Channel debacles of the high summer.

Within a fortnight the units concerned – Hauptmann Paul-Werner

Hozzel's I./StG 1 and Major Walter Enneccerus' II./StG 2 – were being led down the Italian peninsula by the *Geschwaderstab* StG 3, under whose immediate command they were to operate. By 26 December the bulk of the two *Gruppen* had reached Reggio Emilia and Forli respectively (although each was shedding a number of stragglers requiring repair on the way, and trailing in its wake a supply train of Ju 52 transports carrying ground-crews and essential equipment).

On 2 January 1941 the first Ju 87 of the *Stabsstaffel* StG 3 touched down on the dive-bombers' assigned base at Trapani, on the north-west coast of Sicily. The next few days saw the arrival of the two *Gruppen* – some 80 Stukas in all.

The Stukas head south – but unlike I./StG 1 and II./StG 2, who endured appalling visibility during their transfer to Sicily, the Alps are revealed in all their majesty to the pilot of this Ju 87, en route to Italy a year later to conduct carrier arrestor-hook trials with the Italian Navy (note the hook visible just forward of the tailwheel)

Hitler's original intention had been to send X.*Fliegerkorps* to the Mediterranean 'for a limited period only' to attack British ships passing between Sicily and North Africa. And the two *Stukagruppen*, with their reputation for pin-point accuracy (enemy opposition permitting!), had been attached to the *Fliegerkorps* for a very specific purpose. The order which Oberstleutnant Karl Christ, *Kommodore* of StG 3, had been given, and which he now passed on to his two subordinate *Kommandeure*, was straight and to the point – 'The *Illustrious* has got to be sunk'.

This 23,000-ton aircraft carrier was the newest in the Royal Navy, having only joined the Mediterranean Fleet four months earlier. On 11 November 1940 it was aircraft from the *Illustrious* which carried out the now historic raid on the Italian Navy in Taranto harbour, sinking three battleships at their moorings. This action, which effectively 'freed the Mediterranean for the British fleet', also put the *Illustrious* at the top of the Axis' list of targets. The Italians had failed to damage her. Now it was the turn of the Luftwaffe's Stukas.

It was estimated that it would require four direct bomb hits to sink the *Illustrious*. Although no warship of her size had ever been subjected to such punishment, the Stuka crews were confident that they could do the job given the vast expanse of her flightdeck, which offered a target area of well over 6500 square metres. To perfect their tactics, they practised on a floating mock-up of the carrier's outline moored offshore, not far from their Trapani base. But time was not on their side.

On 6 January 1941 the Royal Navy had launched Operation *Excess*, a complex series of convoy movements in both directions which were to be covered by heavy naval units from either end of the Mediterranean. Among the main force sailing from Alexandria in Egypt were the battle-ships *Warspite* and *Valiant* and the carrier *Illustrious*. Four days later they came within range of the Sicilian-based Stukas. Shortly after midday on 10 January the ships' radar screens picked up a large formation of enemy aircraft bearing down on them from the north. The approaching force comprised 43 Ju 87s – Major Enneccerus' II./StG 2 in the van, closely attended by Hauptmann Hozzel's I./StG 1.

A carefully timed low-level strike against *Valiant* by Italian SM 79 torpedo-bombers had drawn off the *Illustrious'* standing combat air patrol of Fulmar fighters. Now ten of the Stukas peeled off to make diversionary dive-bombing attacks on the two battleships. With the latters' anti-aircraft gunners thus fully engaged, and a newly launched patrol of Fulmars still desperately clawing for height, the *Illustrious* was forced to rely solely on her own high-angle batteries for self-protection. But these were unable to pre-

10 January 1941, and the Royal Navy carrier HMS *Illustrious* comes under heavy bombardment from the Stukas of I./StG 1 and II./StG 2

vent the carnage which followed as the Stukas began to circle some 4000 metres above the vessel, each positioning itself ready for the dive.

Adm Cunningham, C-in-C Mediterranean, witnessed the assault from the bridge of the *Warspite*:

'There was no doubt that we were watching complete experts. Formed roughly in a large circle over the fleet, they peeled off one by one when reaching the attacking position. We could not but admire the skill and precision of it all. The attacks were pressed home to point-blank range, and as they pulled out of the dives some were seen to fly along the flight-deck of the *Illustrious* below the level of the funnel . . . at times she became almost completely hidden in a forest of great bomb splashes.'

The first bomb struck the carrier just eight minutes after the initial

Stuka's eye view of the attack. Beneath an umbrella of anti-aircraft fire, the blunt bows of the burning *Illustrious* are clearly visible (bottom left) as she tries to escape further damage. A light cruiser crosses her wake at top right

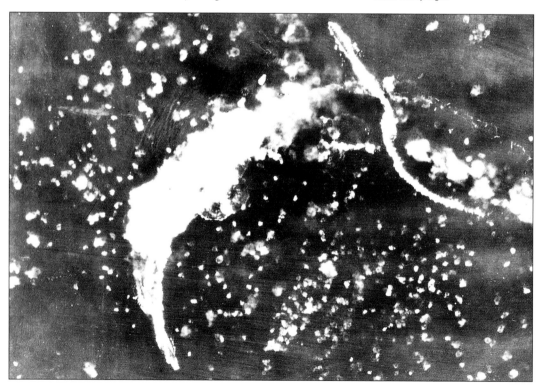

radar sighting. It plunged through a gun position and into the ship's hull to explode at water level. The second hit for'ard close to her bows, and a third demolished another gun mounting alongside her bridge island. The fourth smashed directly on to the descending after lift, wreaking havoc among the aircraft on the hangar deck below and knocking out all the after guns. Incredibly, another pilot placed his bomb down the same after lift well two minutes later, adding to the inferno as ammunition and aviation fuel exploded. A sixth and final bomb tore through the armoured flightdeck before detonating deep inside the ship.

Asked to score four direct hits, the Stukas had in fact delivered no less than six, plus three almost equally damaging near misses (one of which, exploding close alongside, had burst open the for'ard lift, fanning the smoke and flames from the after hangar space like a blowtorch along the full length of the ship). But by some miracle her engines had remained untouched, and while damage control parties fought the fires, the *Illustrious* – steering by main engines only – set course for the dubious haven of Malta. Despite two further attacks she reached the island that same evening and was taken under tow into Valetta dockyard.

Her ordeal was not yet over, but first Enneccerus took time off on 11 January to despatch ten Ju 87s against another naval force sighted retiring eastwards from Malta. At extreme range they caught the cruisers *Southampton* and *Gloucester* by surprise. Attacking out of the sun, the pilots scored hits on both vessels, the former being so badly damaged that she had to be abandoned and sunk by her escorts. Then it was time for the two *Stukagruppen* to turn their attention back to the crippled *Illustrious*.

Over the next 12 days, as naval dockyard workers struggled around the clock to make her seaworthy enough to attempt a dash for the safety of Alexandria, the Stukas, being equally determined that she should not escape, mounted a series of savage raids. On 13 January aircraft of I./StG 1, each weighed down with a single 1000-kg bomb, failed to register a single hit. But in a combined assault flown three days later – the heaviest raid yet experienced by the islanders of Malta – one of the 44 participating Ju 87s planted yet another bomb close to the seemingly ill-fated after lift well.

Like Adm Cunningham before them, many of the anti-aircraft gunners defending Valetta's Grand Harbour expressed grudging admiration for the Stuka pilots' courage and determination in pressing home their attacks:

'I can still see clearly a German bomber diving through that terrific curtain of steel, followed by a Fulmar. The bomber dropped his bomb and proceeded to sneak his way out through the harbour entry only a few inches above the water. He was so low that he had to rise to clear the breakwater, which is only some 15 ft high.'

A column of smoke and dust from another near miss towers over the *Illustrious* – just visible to the right of the large crane – as she undergoes emergency repairs in Malta's Grand Harbour

Another, whose gun emplacement was closer to the *Illustrious'* berth in French Creek, described bombs dropping 'in and around all the creeks, causing terrific clouds of dust, flying masonry and iron' – one of his gun crew swore he saw a complete car sailing through the murk overhead! – 'the dust and spray often blinded our view, but the dive-bombers always came on. As they broke through the dust they seemed like hawks looking for prey'.

On 18 January the Stukas changed their tactics, 51 of them targeting the airfields at Hal Far and Luqa in an obvious attempt to neutralise the island's fighter defences before returning to finish off the *Illustrious*. Twenty-four hours later they were back over the Grand Harbour. Two heavy bombs landed alongside the carrier, hurling her hard against the wharf and holing her under water. But despite this further damage, the naval engineers and dockyard labourers won the battle. On the evening of 23 January the battered *Illustrious* slipped her moorings and crept out to sea. After reaching Alexandria on 25 January, *Illustrious* went on to the USA, where she was to spend nearly a year undergoing extensive repair.

I./StG 1 and II./StG 2 had failed in their mission to sink the *Illustrious*, but at minimal cost to themselves – three aircraft missing from the initial strike on 10 January,y and four recorded losses over Malta since. They had taught their Lordships a salutary lesson in air versus sea power, and for the next two years the Royal Navy rarely risked sending anything larger than a cruiser through the Sicilian Narrows.

The disappearance of capital ships from the central Mediterranean did not mean the end of Stuka activity in the area, however. The Italian and British navies may have withdrawn their battle fleets out of harm's way (each was still digesting their recent experiences at Taranto and off Malta respectively, and had developed a healthy respect for the other side's use of aviation), but the island of Malta itself still sat undefeated astride the sea-lanes linking Italy to the Axis forces in North Africa. There now began an all-out effort to bomb Malta into submission.

The two *Stukagruppen* on Sicily played but a brief part in this renewed offensive. Little more than a week after the *Illustrious'* escape from Malta, Hauptmann Hozzels' I./StG 1 was transferred across the Mediterranean to support the Axis land forces in Libya. II./StG 2 under Major Ennec-cerus followed in their footsteps a fortnight later.

The units selected to replace them at Trapani were the remaining two *Gruppen* of I./StG 1, both currently still languishing in northern France. They had received their movement orders at very short notice. III./StG 1's hectic departure from St Pol was further complicated by the fact that the 'liberated' British Army vehicles which they used for (among other purposes) their *Gruppe* HQ and as mobile workshops, and which they were determined should follow them to Sicily by rail, were too high to go through the Alpine tunnels en route – even with their wheels removed they were still a vital 12 centimetres too tall.

So, when on the morning of 19 February Hauptmann Helmut Mahlke led his 30 Ju 87s on the first leg of their journey south (via Metz to Munich), a team of mechanics was busy with oxy-acetylene torches cutting 15 centimetres off the top of each truck before carefully rewelding its roof back on!

Tragically, the airborne transfer was not made without loss. Two of the

Gruppe's Ju 52 transports flew into mountainsides as bad weather closed in on them after they had departed Munich, whilst a third had a narrow escape – it crash-landed after hitting the power cables which spanned the Brenner Pass (luckily, a quick-thinking electricity official at Innsbruck power station had noticed the transport's course as it flew overhead into the gathering overcast and had turned the current off as a precaution). The Stukas' fortunes were equally mixed. One pilot was killed in a forced landing in

southern Italy after suffering engine failure. Another, finding himself in a similar predicament over mountains, pulled off an amazing landing on a tiny terraced plot of land high on a hillside – more work for the overburdened groundcrew, who had to completely dismantle the machine before it could be retrieved piece by piece from its involuntary eyrie!

Poor visibility was still dogging the *Gruppe* as they finally felt their way in to Trapani on the evening of 23 February. It was not until the following morning, which brought with it a bright blue Mediterranean sky, that they first set eyes on the looming bulk of Monte Erice, which towered some 750 metres above the landscape just north of the field – and realised that they had been extremely lucky not to have suffered even further casualties on landing.

With the arrival, too, of Hauptmann Anton Keil's II./StG 1, the reason for their abrupt departure from France was made clear. Plans were being drawn up to mount a combined German-Italian airborne invasion of Malta. It would be the Stukas' job to prevent the Royal Navy's Mediterranean Fleet from interfering. In the event the scheme was shelved (it reappeared a year later as Operation *Herkules*, before finally being abandoned altogether), the British Fleet remained firmly ensconced in Gibraltar, and the two *Stukagruppen* were redirected to add their weight – and the benefit of their pin-point accuracy – to the ongoing aerial bombardment of the island.

Hauptmann Mahlke had good reason to remember 26 February 1941 and III./StG 1's first mission over Malta. Lifting off from their forward base at Comiso, they set course out to sea escorted by the Bf 109s of 7./JG 26. Every Stuka pilot had been shown reconnaissance photos of their objective – Luqa airfield – and each had been allocated one of the blast pens occupied by a British aircraft as his individual target.

Skirting the anti-aircraft batteries ringing Valetta, the *Gruppe* eased into their line-astern battle formation. This allowed every pilot to locate and identify his particular objective before his turn came to wing into the 70-80° dive on the airfield, which lay some four kilometres to the southwest of the Maltese capital.

Mahlke's own target was located on the eastern edge of the field. After releasing his bomb at the prescribed height of 450 metres, he began to pull out of the dive. Despite the 'light and medium flak firing from every

Planning the next attack on the island, Major Paul-Werner Hozzel, *Gruppenkommandeur* of I./StG 1, confers with the newly-arrived Hauptmann Helmut Mahlke of III./StG 1 in the latter's luxurious (if somewhat low-ceilinged – see text!) ex-British army HQ vehicle at Trapani

barrel and direction', he attempted to line up his wing guns on another target on the far side of the strip. He was over the centre of the runway, still slightly nose-down at a height of some 200 metres, when suddenly;

'A tremendous jolt, an ear-splitting crash, and my right wing burst open. My "Iolanthe" immediately fell away steeply to the right (like many veteran Stuka pilots, Mahlke referred to his Ju 87 as "Iolanthe", a term dating back to the type's operational debut with the *Condor Legion* in Spain – see companion volume *Osprey Combat Aircraft 1 - Ju 87 Stukageschwader 1937-41* for further details). I had automatically yanked the stick back into my stomach and now punched it hard left. It wasn't enough. The middle of my right wing had been blown completely open by a direct flak hit. The wind resistance was so fierce that I could scarcely hold her, even with full left flap and aileron. To make matters worse, I found myself crabbing towards a large hangar!

'Desperately, I trimmed her tail-heavy and applied full throttle. By now I was only four or five metres above the surface of the field and still heading for that hangar. The doors were wide open, and as it grew bigger I could see every detail inside, including three aircraft which, until a few moments ago, had presumably been undergoing repair. "If I go, those three will be going with me", I thought, as I sat there helpless, clutching the stick hard into my left side.

'Slowly "Iolanthe" began to respond. Her nose rose above the horizontal and – almost as if she herself was putting her all into one final leap – we just cleared the hangar roof. But our difficulties were not yet over. In front of us was a hill topped by a line of telegraph poles. Not a very large hill, but in our state it might as well have been Mount Everest. Would we be lucky a second time? We scraped between two poles, our undercarriage taking a length of the wire in passing, and descended into a shallow valley leading southwards towards the coast and open water!'

But further dangers lay ahead, or, more accurately, behind:

'Suddenly, the voice of my gunner, Fritz Baudisch, sounded in my earphones: *"Hurricane coming up into firing position astern!"* I had my hands full just keeping us in the air, and could do nothing except answer as calmly as possible, *"Well, shoot it down then, Fritzchen"*. It was a tall order, one machine-gun against eight, even if Fritz's weapon hadn't chosen that moment to jam after just one short burst.

'"This is it", I thought, as I hunched down in my seat and watched tiny holes appearing in both wings. The Hurricane overshot on his first pass and curved round for a second. Fritz still hadn't cleared the stoppage. But now, quite out of character, he suddenly launched into an excited running commentary from the rear cockpit: *Me 109!! – a long way astern – turning in behind the Hurricane – still miles away – diving at a hell of a rate! The Hurricane's almost within firing distance – the '109's behind him. Still too far away, though. The '109's opened fire – going full pelt and at extreme range – but he's got him!! Still firing. The Hurricane's definitely been hit. He's on fire! He's going in!!"'*

The Hurricane plunged into the sea just behind the Stuka. Postwar research suggests that it was being flown by Flg Off F F 'Eric' Taylor DFC of No 261 Sqn who, at the time, was Malta's leading scorer with seven kills to his credit, and that the Bf 109 pilot who shot him down was Oberleutnant Joachim Müncheberg, *Staffelkapitän* of 7./JG 26 (the Stukas' fighter escort), himself a prominent ace (see *Osprey Aircraft of the Aces 2 - Bf 109Aces of the Mediterranean and North Africa* for further details).

It may, or may not, have been Müncheberg who shot the Hurricane off Mahlke's tail, but when it came to landing the crippled Stuka, the latter was very much on his own;

'Sicily slowly hove into view – Comiso. I had checked "Iolanthe's" controls during the flight back and knew if I eased off the speed even a fraction, she would immediately tip over on to her right wing. The landing would have to be made at full throttle. There was very little wind, but fortunately Comiso was a fairly large field, and with luck we should make it. I quickly gave Fritzchen the usual string of instructions normally issued prior to any crash-landing likely to end up in a somersault – *"Open cabin roof! – tighten harness! – remove goggles! – pull in knees! – arms in front of face! . . . start praying!!"*

'Over the edge of the field I chopped the throttle and switched off the ignition. The aircraft touched down at high speed, landing, as expected, heavily on the right wheel. Luckily the undercarriage held and we proceeded to bounce down the strip, first on one wheel and then the other. After careering two-thirds of the way across the field, we were beginning to slow down and I applied the brakes – gently at first, and then harder. We finally rolled to a stop some 20 metres from the far end of the field. Despite all the damage, the fuel tanks and the tyres had remained unscathed. We'd made it!'

In fact, subsequent inspection revealed that in addition to the flak hit, the Stuka had no fewer than 184 bullet holes in its wings! But others had been less fortunate. One 7.*Staffel* crew went down in the sea some five kilometres off Malta's smaller sister island of Gozo and spent the rest of the war in captivity. Hauptmann Keil's II./StG 1 reported three aircraft missing in the same raid (the heaviest suffered by Malta since the 19 January attack on *Illustrious* in the Grand Harbour) and both *Gruppen* had other aircraft damaged and aircrew wounded.

This set the pattern for the coming weeks as II. and III./StG 1, controlled now by their own *Geschwaderstab* (which had recently replaced Stab StG 3), kept up the pressure on Malta. In the process they suffered a relatively low, but constant, rate of attrition. During the 5 March raid on Hal Far airfield they faced an additional hazard. The attack was to be a combined affair, with Ju 88 high-level bombers following ten minutes in their wake. But the timing went awry and both units arrived over the target simultaneously. Intent on their dives, most of the Stuka crews were fortunately unaware of the carpet of bombs which had formated on them! In the event, no damage was done (to the Stukas, at least), both of the day's Ju 87 losses being as a result of subsequent enemy action.

On 9 April the long-range Ju 87Rs of 7. and 8./StG 1 were trans-

Hauptmann Helmut Mahlke, *Gruppenkommandeur* of III./StG 1, whose first mission against Malta on 26 February 1941 was a salutary introduction to the war in the Mediterranean

The starboard wing of Ju 87B 'J9+AH' – the aircraft Mahlke was flying on 26 February – shows the extent of the damage caused by the direct hit from an anti-aircraft shell. The comments of 'AH's' 'owner', *Staffelkapitän* Hartmut Schairer, upon seeing the state Mahlke had returned his aircraft in are best left unrecorded!

A subsequent tenant of Trapani, this Ju 87R of I./StG 3 returns from a raid on Malta later in the year

ferred to North Africa. This was a temporary measure while II. *Gruppe* remained in Sicily undergoing 'tropicalisation'. Once this process was complete, the two formations exchanged places, 7. and 8. *Staffeln* returning to Trapani early in May. During their absence, 9./StG 1's 'Bertas' had continued to mount sporadic attacks against Malta both by day and by night.

By now the first phase of the aerial onslaught against the island was drawing to a close. There was, however, to be one final flurry of action involving the Ju 87, occasioned by an Allied joint convoy operation designed both to supply Malta and to deliver tanks to the British Army of the Nile. Lasting from 6 to 12 May, it attracted the attention of units of both the German and the Italian air forces, including all three *Gruppen* of *Stukageschwader* 1.

On 8 May 28 aircraft of I./StG 1 (hastily transferred in to Sardinia) attacked the five tank-carrying merchantmen of convoy 'Tiger' to the west of Malta without result. Twenty-four hours, later II. and III. *Gruppen* concentrated once again on the beleaguered island itself. Among their losses was Oberleutnant Ulrich Heinze, *Staffelkapitän* of 9./StG 1, who was shot down by Hurricanes while reportedly engaging a surfaced British submarine some five kilometres outside the Grand Harbour.

Not the start of a dive-bombing attack, but another I./StG 3 machine safely back from Malta making a somewhat steep approach, presumably to avoid the mountains surrounding Trapani

But within a fortnight of 'Tiger's' passage (although one ship had been sunk after hitting a mine at the entrance to the Sicilian Narrows, the other four had made it safely through escorted by naval units including the battleship *Queen Elizabeth*), the last Stukas of StG 1 had vacated Trapani. The focus of the air war in the Mediterranean had shifted eastwards.

'PICCHIATELLI'

Although the name 'Stuka' is synonymous with *Blitzkrieg*, and immediately conjures up pictures of the Luftwaffe in full cry, the Germans had not been the first to employ the Ju 87 in the Mediterranean theatre.

The Italians had developed their own dive-bomber in the late 'thirties. The twin-engined Savoia-Marchetti SM 85 was designed in response to Mussolini's demand for an aircraft capable of sweeping Britain's Mediterranean Fleet out of what the Duce liked to refer to as 'mare nostrum' ('our sea'). At the time of Italy's entry into the war, on 10 June 1940, the SM 85 equipped one *Gruppo*: Capitano Ercolano Ercolani's 96°, based on the island of Pantelleria, almost midway between Sicily and the coast of Tunisia. Operationally, the 'Flying Banana' – so dubbed because of its distinctive upward curvature both fore and aft when viewed in profile – was a total failure.

After nearly a month of inactivity, the SM 85's moment of glory came when three aircraft spent several hours fruitlessly searching for units of the British fleet reported off Malta. This was the 'Flying Banana's' sole contribution to the Italian dictator's dreams of ridding 'his sea' of the enemy's presence. For by now, Pantelleria's climate – fierce heat by day, dampness at night – had done its worst. Parked out in the open, the SM 85s' wooden structures were beginning to warp badly. Still convinced of his air force's need for a dive-bomber, Mussolini turned, not for the last time, to his Axis partner for assistance.

A special mission, headed by Generale Pricolo, Chief of the Italian Air Staff, was despatched to Germany to negotiate the purchase of sufficient Ju 87s initially to equip two full *gruppi*. And before July 1940 was out, the first 15 Italian pilots had arrived at the Luftwaffe's *Stuka-Schule* 2 at Graz-Thalerhof, in Austria, to begin training – a similar number arrived the following month.

The enthusiast below the port wing obviously feels that one of the first Picchiatelli of the *Regia Aeronautica* to arrive at Comiso would make a good subject for a snap or two. Note the Fiat G 50 fighter parked at the extreme right of the photo

This early 96° *Gruppo* machine, anonymous except for a minuscule 549 ahead of the tail cross, still shows signs of its previous ownership. Note this fresh sheen on the fuselage and light patches on the wings where the Luftwaffe markings have been overpainted

Because of the Duce's expressed desire for swift action, these early conversion courses were condensed and accelerated. The German instructors were impressed by their pupils' enthusiasm and élan, and tried to teach them as much as possible in the limited time available. The Italians, for their part (all hand-picked and many of them ex-fighter pilots), greatly appreciated the Stuka's performance and handling characteristics, especially after their recent sorry experience with the SM 85.

The first Italian Ju 87s were not delivered from the factory, but were taken over from the Luftwaffe, their markings simply being overpainted and replaced by those of the *Regia Aeronautica*. This was not the only 'de-Aryanization' that the Stukas underwent, for the Italian crews quickly coined their own name for their new mounts. In an aeronautical context, the Italian word 'picchiata' (a good thrashing) may also be used to indicate a dive. And in any self-respecting dictionary, the next entry will be 'picchiatello', meaning slightly crazy. This happy juxtapositioning – describing both the machine and those who revelled in standing it on its nose and riding it earthwards in near vertical descent – gave the Stuka its new name. Resplendent in freshly-painted Italian insignia, the Ju 87 became the Picchiatello.

Despite forfeiting the sense of dread associated with the word 'Stuka', and now sounding more like a cartoon character, the Ju 87 in Italian hands would prove a potent weapon. But greatly inferior in numbers, it would always remain in the shadow of its German counterparts. Besides, such niceties of nomenclature were completely lost on the enemy. Mirroring the Luftwaffe's 'Spitfire snobbery' of the Battle of Britain then approaching its climax far to the north), every Allied serviceman in the Mediterranean – be he soldier on the ground or sailor at sea – was convinced that the dive-bomber which had singled *him* out as its target was a German Stuka. It has been said that there are no atheists in foxholes, and it would appear that there were very few eagle-eyed pedants either, for there is no recorded instance of an aircraft look-out ever yelling the warning, 'Take cover! *Picchiatelli!*'

Within eight weeks of its one abortive sortie with the SM 85, Capitano Ercolani's re-equipped 96° *Gruppo* had resumed operational readiness. Based at Comiso, in south-eastern Sicily, its two subordinate *squadriglie*, 236[a] and 237[a], now had a combined strength of fifteen Ju 87s. Their arrival coincided with that of the new British aircraft carrier *Illustrious*, which first entered the Mediterranean on 31 August. Two days later off Malta, the *Illustrious* underwent her baptism of fire by dive-bombers when a total of thirteen Picchiatelli attacked her in two separate raids. It proved to be an inconclusive affair, despite both sides' claiming successes – the Italians' reported hits on a carrier and an escorting cruiser, whilst the ship's gunners were convinced they had shot down five of the attackers.

Forty-eight hours later still, on 4 September 1940, the island of Malta

A large cloud of smoke and Maltese dust rises above Hal Far airfield – Mikabba to the Italians – as it comes under attack by 96° *Gruppo*'s Picchiatelli

itself, which had been experiencing high-level aerial bombardment by the *Regia Aeronautica* since the opening day of hostilities, suffered its first dive-bombing raid. Unable to locate merchant shipping reported in Valetta's Grand Harbour, five Ju 87s of 96° *Gruppo* turned their attention instead on Fort Delimara some ten kilometres to the south.

Several more raids followed before the month was out. On 15 September a dozen Picchiatelli took off from Comiso to bomb Hal Far airfield. They were accompanied on this mission by the prototype SM 86, flown by Savoia-Marchetti's chief test pilot, Maresciallo Elio Scarpini. This was a refined and re-engined development of the company's earlier SM 85 and although it bore little in common with the disastrous 'Flying Banana', Scarpini's post-operational report on the SM 86's performance was far from encouraging.

On 17 September the Ju 87s returned to Malta, and this time their target was Luqa airfield. The bombing was described by an eye-witness on the ground as '. . . remarkably good. They hit practically every hangar'. They also destroyed a Wellington which had just landed en route to Cairo. But this raid was to cost the 96° their first combat casualties. Attacked by Hurricanes, one 237ª *Squadriglia* machine came down in the sea near the tiny island of Filfla, whilst another Picchiatello returned to Comiso with a dead gunner on board.

This was 96° *Gruppo*'s last appearance of the year over Malta, for Mussolini had his sights firmly fixed elsewhere. He had already adopted Hitler's expansionist tactics once before when he occupied Albania in the spring of 1939. Now he emulated his Axis partner yet again by issuing his next intended victim, Greece, with an impossible ultimatum that was nothing more than a pretext for aggression. Presented to the Greek government at 3 am on the morning of 28 October 1940, this document, containing such phrases as '. . . all these provocations can no longer be tolerated . . .', could have been penned by the Führer himself.

17

As expected, the Duce's ultimatum was rejected out of hand by the Greeks, and within hours the Italian troops massed in Albania had crossed the Greek frontier in three main columns – one heading east for Salonika, another for Yannina, in the mountains of Epirus, and the third south along the coast to isolate the offshore island of Corfu, which had for many years been one of Mussolini's most coveted objectives.

To support this triple thrust, the *Regia Aeronautica*'s presence in the area was reinforced, not only in occupied Albania itself, but also in Italy's south-eastern 'heel', which was only some 100 kms away across the Straits of Otranto. Among the units moved up into the latter region was Capitano Ercolani's 96° *Gruppo*. His two *squadriglie*, operating a mix of twenty Ju 87Bs and Rs, departed Comiso for Lecce in the latter half of October 1940.

For the first four days of the invasion all went according to plan. But Greek resistance was rapidly hardening, and on 1 November they launched a counter-offensive which stopped the Italian drive on Florina – the first objective on the road to Salonika – dead in its tracks. Worse still for the Duce's dreams of an easy conquest, his troops were pushed back across the border as the Greeks drove towards the Albanian town of Koritza, the advanced supply base of the Italian army. After just 96 hours the invaders had become the invaded.

96° *Gruppo*'s first raids across the Straits of Otranto were mounted on 2 November when six Ju 87Bs attacked Corfu and five of their larger-range R-models struck further inland at Yannina. Two days later they were back over Yannina, accompanied once more by Elio Scarpini in the twin-engined SM 86. This time the test pilot's report was even more damming, and the type was quietly withdrawn. Savoia-Marchetti later had one more crack at producing an indigenous dive-bomber for the Duce, the single-engined SM 93 being unusual in that the pilot was accommodated in a prone position to prevent his blacking-out when pulling out of the dive. Completed in 1943, the sole prototype was tested for the Luftwaffe before it, too, was abandoned.

A bombed-up Ju 87 of the new 97° *Gruppo* displays its *squadriglia* number in black on the white fuselage band. Note also the original Luftwaffe Wk-Nr (5792) at the top of the tailfin

Meanwhile, the Italians' plight along the Greco-Albanian border was worsening. Despite strong air support, which included 96° *Gruppo*'s bombing of bridges and Greek artillery positions, the Duce's troops continued to retreat on Koritza. The town fell to the Greeks on 23 November.

It was at this juncture that a second Ju 87-equipped dive-bomber *Gruppo* was added to the *Regia Aeronautica*'s order of battle. After final working up at Lonate Pozzolo in the north of Italy, the first Picchiatelli

of 97° *Gruppo* began to stage southwards. They arrived at Comiso, in Sicily, to replace the 96° *Gruppo* (which had departed for Lecce a month earlier) on 11 November 1940. But it was another fortnight before the new 97° *Gruppo* – commanded by Maggiore Antonio Moscatelli and comprising the 238ª and 239ª *Squadriglie* – was declared fully operational.

On 28 November they carried out their first mission – an abortive attack on Royal Navy vessels, reportedly the cruiser *Glasgow* and her attendant destroyers, sighted west of Malta. But they had time to do little more in the central Mediterranean area before they were also sucked into the war in Albania.

For by now Mussolini's grand offensive was in ruins. The central and western columns of the original three-pronged plan of attack had likewise been driven back into their 'own' territory. In the Epirus mountains the Albanian town of Argyrokastron – another major Italian base – was captured by the Greeks on 4 December, and 48 hours later they took Santi Quaranta, a small but important supply harbour on the coast road some 10 kms inside Albania.

It was against this coastal strip and the mountains immediately beyond that the Picchiatelli concentrated their efforts for the remainder of the year. Having joined 96° *Gruppo* at Lecce on 6 December, the newcomers

of 97° *Gruppo* mounted their first two strikes against targets along the coast road north of Corfu eight days later. On 19 December it was 96° *Gruppo*'s turn; one small vessel being claimed sunk after twenty-four aircraft dive-bombed Santi Quaranta (until recently this had been one of their own ports of supply which, during their occupation of Albania, the Italians had renamed Port Edda in honour of Mussolini's daughter, Countess Ciano). 21 December saw 96° *Gruppo* back over Albania attacking Greek posi-

This pair of Picchiatelli also belong to 97° *Gruppo*, as witness the telltale white shape on the machines' wheel spats . . .

. . . which on this later machine of the same *gruppo* is seen more clearly to be the unit emblem – a diving white duck attacking a ship 'sailing' along the bottom edge of the spat (see colour profile No 35)

19

tions in the mountains. But on each of the two separate raids carried out that day the *Gruppo* lost a Ju 87 to anti-aircraft fire. As ill-luck would have it, one of the missing pilots was Savoia-Marchetti's Maresciallo Elio Scarpini, who had gone along on yet another operational sortie.

Such losses were rare, however. And of those which were suffered, nearly all were as a result of ground fire, for by the very nature of their missions – a seaward approach to the target, followed by retirement back over open water immediately afterwards – the Picchiatelli seldom encountered the sort of enemy fighter opposition being met by the Albanian-based units of the *Regia Aeronautica.*

By this stage the Duce's 'private war' had escalated. He had been forced to turn once again to Germany for help, and Ju 52 transports of the Luftwaffe were being employed to augment his lines of supply across the Adriatic. The Greeks, too, had sought assistance. When the invasion was only hours old, they had appealed to Britain to honour the guarantee given to them by Prime Minister Chamberlain at the time Italy first seized control of Albania. And unlike the hapless Poles, who had been in a similar situation some 14 months earlier and had received nothing but rhetoric from the British Government, the Greek plea was answered. Material aid was sent in by sea and air, British troops landed on Greek soil, and RAF squadrons were despatched to fight alongside the heavily outnumbered Greek Air Force.

In the first week of the new year, Italian reconnaissance aircraft reported a marked increase in Royal Navy activity at both ends of the Mediterranean. They rightly deduced that this heralded another major Allied convoy. It was, in fact, Operation *Excess*, the complicated movement of shipping from either end of the Mediterranean mentioned at the beginning of the previous chapter. And its most important component was undoubtedly the fast military convoy of four merchantmen – one bound for Malta and three bringing aid to Greece – which sailed from Gibraltar on 6 January 1941.

Part of the Axis response was a build-up of air power in Sicily. Leaving 97° *Gruppo* to carry on the war in Albania, the more experienced 96° was therefore withdrawn from Lecce and returned to Comiso on 8 January. The next day they participated in Malta's first air raid of the new year when nine of their Picchiatelli attacked Kalafrana. And twenty-four hours

A Ju 87R of 208a *Squadriglia*, 101° *Gruppo*, photographed in the relatively enemy fighter-free Albanian skies

Bomb-laden Picchiatelli of 208a
***Squadriglia* en route to a target on**
the Albanian Front . . .

later it was a trio of aircraft from 96° *Gruppo*'s 236ª *Squadriglia* which carried out one of the two dive-bombing attacks on the carrier *Illustrious* as she limped towards Malta after her ordeal at the hands of the Luftwaffe's Stukas.

This very first example of a combined German-Italian dive-bomber operation – 40+ Stukas followed up by just three Picchiatelli – was all too typical of what was to come in the months ahead. Far fewer in numbers, the Italian pilots, through no fault of their own, would find themselves overshadowed (except in their own national press!) by their German comrades in arms. Although individual exploits and personalities would shine through, when Capitano Ercolani's 96° *Gruppo* arrived at Castel Benito, in Libya, at the beginning of February 1941 to fight alongside I./StG 1 and II./StG 2 in North Africa, it was very much as a junior partner.

Meanwhile, 97° *Gruppo* continued to face the rigours of the Albanian campaign. On 9 February one of their aircraft was damaged in a rare encounter with Greek fighters. But it was that old enemy, anti-aircraft fire, which brought down another machine over the frontlines two days later – several others suffered AA (anti-aircraft artillery) hits during this period. It was at this time that two more *squadriglie* – 208ª and 209ª – were formed to make up for the absence of 96° *Gruppo* now in Africa. Their arrival at Lecce led to some organisational changes, the newly-established 209ª taking 238ª *Squadriglia*'s slot in 97° *Gruppo*.

Early in March 1941 the displaced 238ª was transferred from Lecce to Tirana, in Albania. Here, it paired with 208ª *Squadriglia* to form the new 101° *Gruppo*. More than four months after their invasion of Greece, the Italian troops on the Albanian front finally had some effective tactical air support!

Remaining at Lecce, 97° *Gruppo* (now comprising 209ª and 239ª *Squadriglie*) continued to mount raids across the Straits of Otranto. On 22 March the 'old hands' of the 239ª caught a convoy off Corfu, claiming one ship sunk and a second damaged. One of 97° *Gruppo*'s most senior pilots, Capitano Guiseppe Cenni, had recently devised a new method of attacking surface vessels. Accepting the fact that the Picchiatello was never likely to be available in sufficient numbers to permit the *Regia Aeronautica* to stage the classic style Stuka attack perfected by the Luftwaffe – a continuous succession of aircraft diving steeply from a high altitude and from all points of the compass to confuse and overwhelm the enemy's defences – Cenni opted

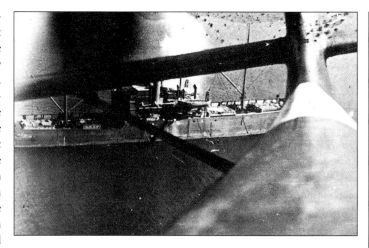

The 'Cenni Method' of attacking shipping, as demonstrated by 239a *Squadriglia* against a merchantman off the North African coastline

instead for a shallow high-speed dive down to very low level. The bomb would then be released in horizontal flight, its forward momentum causing it to 'bounce' across the surface of the water (rather like a flat stone flipped across a pond) before smashing into the target's hull and exploding.

In effect, what Cenni had done was to pre-empt by many months both the 'skip-bombing' technique later used to such effect by the Americans in the south-west Pacific, and the even more famous (and admittedly more sophisticated) 'bouncing bomb' developed by Barnes Wallis for the 'Dambusters' raid of May 1943.

One of the first recorded victims of the 'Cenni Method' of attack was the 932-ton Greek freighter *Susanna*, sunk by Cenni himself with a direct hit off the coast of Corfu on 4 April. In admitting the loss, the Greeks – deceived by the low level of the attack–- ascribed it to 'aircraft torpedo'! And in a repeat performance during the third and final raid on enemy shipping off Corfu that same day, 239ª *Squadriglia* caught the Greek navy's *Poussa*, claiming it as a destroyer, although she was, in fact, a small World War 1-vintage gunboat of some 240 tons!

These sinkings effectively represented the swan-song of the Picchiatello as an independent participant in the Mediterranean theatre of war, for less than 48 hours later Hitler's troops invaded the Balkans.

Numbered among the Luftwaffe's supporting air armada were more than 250 Stukas. In contrast to the latters' steamroller advance through Yugoslavia and Greece, the part played in the campaign by the *Regia Aeronautica*'s two dive-bomber *gruppi* was, at best, peripheral. Never able to field more than a fraction of the strength available to the German *Gruppen*, and continuing to be wholly reliant upon their Axis partner for spares and equipment, the Picchiatelli would find themselves cast in a subordinate role throughout much of their remaining operational career.

The engine tarpaulin is removed from an unidentified Ju 87R in readiness for the day's operations

OPERATIONS *MARITA AND MERKUR*

By conquering Greece, Mussolini had hoped to present Hitler with a *fait accompli* and prove himself an equal partner in the Axis alliance. In fact, many have since argued that his precipitate action planted the first seeds of the Führer's ultimate downfall. Hitler had known nothing of Mussolini's intentions. When he first learned of the Duce's invasion of Greece he was horrified. He had already driven one British Expeditionary Force from the mainland of Europe less than four months earlier at Dunkirk. And now – with plans for an invasion of the Soviet Union uppermost in his own mind – the last thing he wanted was a similar force establishing a toe-hold in the Balkans perilously close to his main source of fuel, the oilfields of Rumania.

But after five months of nothing but reversals in Albania, defeat was staring Mussolini in the face. To rescue his partner-in-arms and stabilise the situation in south-eastern Europe, the Führer's plans for Russia were perforce put on hold. First he would have to neutralise Greece and push the British back into the sea, '. . . they retreated quickly enough the last time we let our Panzers and Stukas loose on them. No doubt they'll do the same again!', he boasted at the time

The only other Balkan nation not already firmly in the Axis camp was Greece's immediate northern neighbour, Yugoslavia. Here, diplomatic pressure was applied. On 25 March 1941 representatives of the Yugoslav government signed the Tripartite Pact in Vienna. With Yugoslav subservience assured, the way was now clear for Operation *Marita* – the German invasion of Greece. But within 48 hours a popular uprising in Yugoslavia had toppled the government, deposed the Prince Regent and proclaimed the teenaged Peter as King. Although the new régime was careful not to provoke the Axis, this sudden reversal of policy to one of strict neutral-

The transfer to the Balkans did not always go smoothly. Here, on an overcrowded field, a Ju 52 transport of IV./KGzbV 1 has rolled into a line of parked Stukas

ity had thwarted Hitler's carefully laid plans. An enraged Führer immediately ordered that *Marita* be expanded to include a simultaneous attack on Yugoslavia.

Among the Luftwaffe units concentrated in south-east Europe for the forthcoming twin invasions of Greece and Yugoslavia were all six remaining *Stukagruppen* from northern France. As part of *General der Flieger* von Richthofen's VIII. *Fliegerkorps* – the main strike force aimed at southern Yugoslavia and Greece (and the Command, incidentally, which had first established the Stuka's terrifying reputation in Poland) – elements of StG 2 had begun leaving the Channel coast as far back as early January. After leisurely stop-overs in both Austria and Rumania, the *Geschwader* reached its assigned bases in Bulgaria in the first week of March 1941. Stab, I. and III./StG 2 were deployed at Krainici and Belica, the latter field also accommodating I./StG 3, which filled the slot left by II./StG 2's current absence in Africa.

Strangely, this first II./StG 2 never did serve under its own *Geschwaderstab* for when it was decided just prior to the start of hostilities in the Balkans to reinforce StG 2 with one of the two African *Stukagruppen*, it was I./StG 1 which – for some reason – was selected to make the journey north across the Mediterranean to Bulgaria.

In contrast to Major Oskar Dinort's StG 2, which had even found the time to take part in a parade and to stage a bombing display for King Boris and his entourage after their arrival in Bulgaria, the transfer of the *Stukageschwader* charged with opening the assault on northern Yugoslavia was a much more hurried affair. The three *Gruppen* of Major Clemens Graf von Schönborn-Wiesentheid's StG 77 were not pulled out of Normandy until *after* the Yugoslav coup of 27 March. Within the week, however, they were in position – Stab, I. and III./StG 77 at Arad, in Rumania, and II./StG 77 (temporarily commanded by Stab StG 3) at Graz, in Austria.

The invasion of Yugoslavia began at 05.15 hours on 6 April 1941 with German ground troops crossing the Bulgarian border and advancing on Nis and Skoplje. Three-quarters of an hour later Reichsminister Doktor

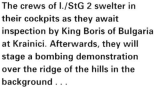

The crews of I./StG 2 swelter in their cockpits as they await inspection by King Boris of Bulgaria at Krainici. Afterwards, they will stage a bombing demonstration over the ridge of the hills in the background . . .

. . . but it's soon back to business as usual, with the Stukas widely dispersed as a precaution against surprise enemy air attack

Ju 87Bs of I./StG 3 at Belica-North, in Bulgaria, await the launch of Operation *Marita*

Not all casualties were caused by enemy action. Oberleutnant Uhlitz, Major Oskar Dinort's *Geschwader-Adjutant*, was killed in a mid-air collision with his wingman near Krainici

Goebbels solemnly announced the declaration of war. Although StG 2's four subordinate *Gruppen* were heavily involved in the south from the outset, it was events to the north which became the focus of world attention. On 3 April the Yugoslavs had declared their capital, Belgrade, an open city. But Hitler was not to be appeased. Determined that Yugoslavia, which had had the effrontery to defy him, should be 'pulverised with merciless brutality'. He ordered a series of devastating raids on Belgrade. It was, perhaps, a sign of his unabated anger that these raids were to be carried out under the code name Operation *Strafgericht* (Punishment).

Shortly before 7 am on that cloudless Palm Sunday morning the Luftwaffe began to destroy Belgrade. There were over 300 aircraft in the first wave, nearly a quarter of them Stukas of StG 77. With their ability to hit pin-point targets, it would appear that the dive-bombers, at least, were assigned specific objectives, as this anonymous Ju 87 pilot subsequently related;

'After the green hedgerows of the Normandy countryside, the warm browns and greys of the local landscape were still unfamiliar to our eyes. The morning sun was glinting off the peaks of the Transylvanian Alps at our backs as we approached the unmistakable silvery ribbon of the Danube, the frontier between Rumania and Yugoslavia. The hazy outlines of a large city appeared in the distance – Belgrade!

'Below us the first few bursts of enemy flak. But nothing to worry about. Those of us who'd been through Poland and France had seen much worse. The city was much clearer now. The white tower-like apartment blocks bright in the morning sun. The *Staffeln* opened out as the pilots prepared to dive. Our target was the fortress which gave the city its name. Perched high above the promontory where the Sava joins the Danube, it could not be missed.

'I felt the jolt as our bomb was released. We levelled out and turned back for base at high speed, ready to prepare for the next mission. As we retired I saw the fortress ringed in smoke and flames. Fires had also been started in the royal palace and the nearby main railway station. Soon smoke hung over the whole city like a grey shroud.'

The raids would go on for days. But while the high-level bombers of *Luftflotte* 4 continued to inflict Hitler's 'punishment' on Belgrade, StG 77's Stukas were soon diverted against Yugoslav Air Force bases and other military targets outside the city and beyond.

A neutral observer witnessed StG 77's attack on Zemun civil and military airfield on the banks of the Sava some five kilometres west of the capital later that same afternoon:

'They approached in single file, about a mile apart. The leading plane circled once over the airport and then dived. It seemed to keep going straight down at three or four hundred miles an hour until its nose was within a few inches of the ground. Then it straightened out and glided away. One plane after another did that. It was all as mechanically perfect, as systematic, and as well timed as if they had been robots.

'Each plane had its own target. Mostly they were dropping bombs on a lot of Yugoslav fighter planes and a few bombers parked on the field. But some of them dropped incendiaries on the hangars and the other airport buildings. Then, after all the bombs had been unloaded, they came back, flying just off the ground, and machine-gunned the men trying to put out the fires or get planes off the ground.

'When they finally left, the whole field was dotted with globs of fire where the Yugoslav machines were burning. Thick black smoke was going up from the buildings.'

Although it was the bombing of Belgrade that made the world's headlines (which was hardly surprising, given the number of foreign correspondents sent in to cover recent events who were caught up in the raids), it was the fighting in the south of the country which decided Yugoslavia's fate. Surrounded on three sides by unfriendly powers, the previous

The battered remains of one of Belgrade's modern apartment blocks following Operation *Punishment*

I./StG 3 over mountainous country along the Yugoslav border

Yugoslav government had spread its seven understrength armies along the entire lengths of its borders. Sufficient perhaps to have deterred local incursions, it was a recipe for disaster when faced with the full weight of a German *Blitzkrieg*. Once this thin outer crust was broken, the inner regions were literally defenceless.

If anywhere, Yugoslav defences were slightly stronger in the north, for it was here, across the German (Austrian) and Hungarian borders and into the flat plainland of Croatia – ideal tank country – that attack seemed most likely. But the Wehrmacht again employed the same surprise tactics which had led to the fall of France the previous year, only this time, instead of debouching out of the 'impenetrable' wooded valleys of the Ardennes into the enemy's rear, the armoured spearheads of the 12. *Armee* erupted out of the ravines and passes of the mountains 'guarding' Yugoslavia's south-eastern frontier with Bulgaria.

It was the task of von Richthofen's VIII. *Fliegerkorps* to cover their advance across lower Yugoslavia to link up with the Italians in Albania. Still paralleling the campaign in the west 11 months earlier (which had seen the British split from the French by the Panzers' thrust to the Channel, after which both forces were defeated separately), this would drive a wedge between the Yugoslavs to the north and the Greeks in the south. But first Stukas of Major Dinort's StG 2 had to knock out the fortifications dominating the all-important passes through the mountains. A tank gunner awaiting the order to advance watched them do it;

'A fine coating of dew covered the vehicles. Only a thin strip of slowly lightening sky above the mountains heralded the start of a new day. It was 5 am on the morning of 6 April. We looked at our watches. Fifteen minutes to go. As we adjusted our binoculars, a pale dawn light started to seep down the hillside in front of us. The mountains behind rose out of a milky white morning mist. One more minute. There! To the west a machine-gun rattled briefly. Then a muffled explosion. A few seconds of complete silence and then the whole front erupted into noise. Our own light flak units added to the din of the artillery.

'Despite the racket, my ears picked up the thin drone of aircraft engines, growing louder by the second. I knew from experience what it was, and pointed the glasses upwards. Sure enough, the dim shapes of approaching Stukas. Now they were circling above us, the dark red pinpoints of their position lights plainly visible beneath the shadows of their wings.

'They slowly began to climb, breaking into the clear light of the new day. More and more aircraft joined them as they headed towards the ridge of mountains immediately to our front. One last circle, as if to make doubly sure of the target below, and then the first *Ketten* went into their dives. Even from here we could hear the familiar nerve-shattering howl of their sirens. And then the first bombs fell. The tiny black specks rained down on the enemy's positions. The noise of the explosions echoed back from unseen clefts in the mountains as *Staffel* after *Staffel* attacked. Soon pillars of yellow-brown smoke were staining the pristine whiteness of the high snowfields.'

Even as this first wave of Stukas was returning to its bases around the Bulgarian capital of Sofia, others were setting out to raid targets up to 100 kms inside Yugoslav territory. Despite being in the air almost continu-

StG 77 moved into Yugoslavia in the wake of the invading ground forces. Here at Prilep a local youth, and his donkey, seem a little nonplussed by all the activity going on around them

A fully-loaded 97° *Gruppo* Picchiatello pictured over Scutari on the Albanian-Yugoslav border. Note the duck emblem on the wheel spat, the yellow theatre nose-band and the addition of an Italian serial number below the German original at the top of the tailfin

ously, StG 2's losses at the close of this first day's fighting were remarkably light – two aircraft lost and two damaged. But they had done the job demanded of them. The leading elements of 12. *Armee* had quickly broken through the thin shell of the Yugoslav 5th Army. By mid-morning German spearheads were over 40 kms beyond the mountain barrier. With little to stand in their way, the Panzers fanned out. Skoplje, halfway to the Albanian border, fell to the 2. and 9. Panzer divisions within 24 hours. *Panzergruppe* 1 turned north. Rattling along the tracks of the Orient Express, they captured Nis on 9 April and headed for Belgrade.

Yugoslavia was *in extremis*. Like a mortally wounded quarry set upon by a pack of hunting dogs, she was now under attack from all sides. To the south-west Italian forces in Albania were no longer on the defensive. Ju 87s of the Tirana-based 101° *Gruppo* began to strike at Yugoslav targets. So too did 97° *Gruppo* at Lecce. Nine Picchiatelli of 239ª *Squadriglia* had crossed the Adriatic Sea on the first afternoon of hostilities to attack the harbour of Kotor, where they lost one of their number to Yugoslav AA fire. On 10 April the *squadriglia*'s long-range Ju 87Rs transferred further northwards up the Italian Adriatic to Iesi. From here they mounted several raids along the Yugoslav Dalmatian coast, attacking enemy torpedo-boats off Sibenik, damaging the 1870-ton seaplane-tender *Zmaj*, and losing more crews to enemy anti-aircraft gunners in the process.

Meanwhile, 101° *Gruppo* was concentrating on targets inland, where they also suffered casualties from ground fire. During an attack on the Mostar airfields on 13 April the Ju 87 of the *gruppo*'s commander, Maggiore Guiseppe Donadio, was hit and forced to land in enemy territory. He and his gunner spent an uncomfortable few days in captivity before being liberated. At least one more 101° Picchiatello was shot down, and four others damaged, by Yugoslav AA batteries along the Albanian frontier.

In the far north-west the Italian 2nd Army was advancing on Ljubljana. Due north, its German namesake had crossed the Austrian border and was heading for Zagreb, where the troops were greeted not as invaders but as liberators. Both Slovenia and Croatia immediately declared their independence from the central Serb government, which had long fled Belgrade for Sarajevo.

To the north-east the Hungarian 3rd Army was reclaiming disputed border territory, while in the east a

A *squadriglia* of Italian Ju 87s cruises serenely at altitude over the inhospitable terrain of central Yugoslavia

One of the cupolas of Fort Istibel, the strongest position within the Metaxas Line, built to guard the Greek-Yugoslav frontier. These small hardened sites could be hit with a fair degree of accuracy by a competent Ju 87 pilot

German army corps advanced out of Rumania towards Belgrade. They entered the Yugoslav capital on 12 April, just beating the leading elements of *Panzergruppe* 1 racing up from Bulgaria. Under attack from all points of the compass, Yugoslavia surrendered on 17 April. The Luftwaffe's Stukas had played little part in the final stages of the campaign against the Yugoslavs, for at 16.00 hours on 15 April the C-in-C *Luftflotte* 4, Generaloberst Alexander Löhr, had received fresh instructions from Reichsmarschall Göring. He was to divert his forces southwards against British troops already beginning their long retreat through Greece. Göring's orders were that they were to be destroyed before they could reach the southern ports and be evacuated by sea. There was to be no second Dunkirk!

GREECE

Unlike the Yugoslavs, the Greeks had at least been accorded the military courtesy of a formal declaration of war, albeit only 30 minutes before Wehrmacht forces began their offensive at 06.00 hours on 6 April 1941. As in Yugoslavia, however, the initial assault would first have to overcome a major mountain barrier. In fact the Greek border with Bulgaria was protected by part of the same range which divided Bulgaria from Yugoslavia. Along its peaks, the Greeks had constructed the Metaxas Line, a 200 km-long string of frontier fortifications. The largest of these was Fort Istibei, which guarded the one main route through the mountains – the Rupel Pass in the valley of the River Struma.

The Germans had christened the Fort Istibei position 'Fortress Mountain'. And in a re-run of the opening attack on the mountain defences of Yugoslavia, flown some 45 minutes earlier, it was again the job of *Stukastaffeln* of Major Dinort's StG 2 to neutralise the enemy forts overlooking the Panzers' line of advance. A war correspondent flew in the leading aircraft of the second wave;

'Now it was our turn to take-off. As we climbed I could make out those behind us – small dots trailing long banners of dust behind them as they accelerated across the surface of the field. As they gained height to formate on us they looked like dark fishes swimming through the morning haze. Closing up in *Ketten* formation, we continued to climb. Spread out ahead of us were the mountains of Macedonia. We set course for Fortress Mountain. Rising from it, a long grey-blue column of smoke was spreading northwards, blown by the wind. Large fires were burning in the enemy positions and a bright red wall of flame was eating through the thick undergrowth on the Greek side of the mountain.

'I did not have time to notice much else. *'Dive!'* yelled the pilot. I quickly grabbed the cabin cross-struts in both hands and braced my feet. The aircraft was already standing on its nose, the tail pointing up into the blue sky. For a second we seemed to hang there in space. Then the force of the dive pressed me hard into the seat. In front of us, framed in the windscreen and growing larger every second – Fortress Mountain!

'We hurtled downwards towards some small grey squares. These must be the bunkers. My whole body was quivering, the wings of the aircraft vibrated with a noise like ghostly metal drums, and my ears were filled with a high-pitched screaming and whistling. Suddenly, a tremendous jolt and I felt a wave of dizziness – the pilot was pulling out of the dive. The pressure in my head and ears slowly eased – I could breathe freely again. Below us the bombs streaked towards their target. We were already several hundred metres away when they exploded, sending huge fountains of earth and debris high into the air between the bunkers.'

Despite this raid, and many others like it, the Greeks resisted stubbornly. For 48 hours practically the whole line held fast. Some lower positions down in the valley were overrun, but the two main forts dominating the Rupel Pass – Istibei and Ussita – repulsed persistent attacks by ground troops and dive-bombers. Two other forts captured on 8 April were retaken almost immediately by Greek counter-attacks.

But like France's vaunted Maginot Line, the Metaxas Line had one weakness – it could be outflanked. On that same 8 April, while the Metaxas defenders were grimly holding their positions in the mountains, German troops swept through Yugoslavia and into Greece behind them. Tanks of 2. *Panzerdivision* entered Salonika on the Aegean coast as darkness fell. Completely cut off from the rest of the country, all Greek forces in the north-eastern provinces were instructed to surrender the following day. In his victory speech, Adolf Hitler had a special word of praise for those Greeks who had been manning the Metaxas Line and who, for three long days, had defied all attempts to dislodge them – 'You are the only troops ever to have held out in this manner under Stuka attack'.

Meanwhile, a second line of defence had been established. Occupied by two Greek divisions and the newly-arrived 'Forces of the Empire', it was anchored firmly on the Gulf of Salonika in the east and stretched some 100 kms through Veria and Edessa to the Yugoslav border . . . where it, too, ended in thin air! Between it and the main body of the Greek Army to the north-west (some two-thirds of which was still locked in the fighting in Albania) was the so-called Monastir Gap. It had been confidently anticipated that the Yugoslav Army would be able to hold its own here in the mountains of southern Serbia. But the inevitable happened. The Germans exploited the gap, and by 11 April Imperial and Greek forces were retreating to yet another line south of Mount Olympus. Here it was the same again. Greek troops on the open left flank, having been fought

The northern elements of StG 77 pushed down through Yugoslavia and into Greece, staging through wreck-littered enemy airfields along the way

More casualties were being suffered through accidents than by enemy action. Here, a Stuka has overturned after running into a rain-eroded gully on a makeshift landing strip

almost to a standstill, were driven back. A third withdrawal was ordered, to the Thermopylae line.

By now the Greeks were on the verge of collapse. On 22 April their Northern Army capitulated to Generalfeldmarschall List's 12. *Armee*. In the Epirus to the north-west, the Greek troops who had advanced into Albania the previous winter finally surrendered there to the Italians. For the Picchiatelli of 97° *Gruppo* at Lecce, the campaign against the Greeks in Albania ended as it had begun with raids across the Straits of Otranto. On 20 and 21 April they mounted several attacks against enemy troop columns on the coast road and on merchant shipping in the Bay of Corfu, during the course of which Guiseppe Cenni again demonstrated his mastery of the 'bouncing bomb' tactic by sinking another Greek steamer, the 1102-ton *Ioanna*.

But these were mere pinpricks compared to events currently unfolding down the eastern half of Greece. Here, British troops and the 'Forces of the Empire' – the latter having readopted their better-known World War 1 acronym ANZACs (Australian and New Zealand Army Corps) on 12 April – were being subjected to relentless and concentrated Stuka attack. For by this time, too, Göring's orders that Allied forces in Greece were to be destroyed before they could escape were being carried out to the letter.

During the first week of the Greek campaign Stuka losses had been relatively light. One of StG 2's first casualties had been Oberleutnant Bruno Dilley of the attached I./StG 1. Shot down over Macedonia on 7 April, Dilley, whose raid on the Dirschau bridge in Poland had opened World War 2, survived

Visible behind this Bf 109E of II./StG 27 is a group of StG 2's Stukas and – half hidden by the fighter's lower propeller blade – one of Major Dinort's *Geschwaderstab* Do 17s. Several of these Dorniers were lost on reconnaissance missions in the opening days of *Marita*

A I./StG 3 reconnaissance photo of vessels off the Megara evacuation beach, including one annotated as a 4000-ton tanker on fire

together with his gunner to return to his unit several days later. In fact, in these early stages, Major Dinort appears to have suffered more damage to his *Stabsstaffel* Do 17 reconnaissance machines then to his dive-bombers.

But after the fall of Yugoslavia and the transfer of the bulk of StG 77 down to the Greek front to join StG 2, the Stukas began to pay a steady, if not exorbitant, price in aircraft lost to, or damaged by, enemy fighters and anti-aircraft fire.

Despite the constant and savage attentions of a Stuka force still totalling over 150 aircraft, British and ANZAC troops continued doggedly to withdraw southwards across the mountains and plains of eastern Greece. The ANZACs, in particular, fought a masterly series of rearguard actions, as witness this somewhat bland official communiqué issued from GHQ Cairo;

'The withdrawal has been covered by Australian and New Zealand troops, whose delaying action has been brilliantly conducted, causing the enemy heavy casualties.'

Someone on the spot put it much more colourfully;

'That evening the Germans massed about 90 dive-bombers. After them the German tanks and infantry would advance. Diving, screechingly low, the Stukas came in squadrons, wave following wave. Columns of earth gushed skyward. The immense ramparts of rock shuddered. Reverberations rolled away among the mountains.

'Under the yellow-painted snouts of the Nazi Junkers, under the tracks of the Panzer forces, the ANZACs pulled their tin hats down over their eyes, dug in deeply, waited, survived, and then inflicted heavy losses on the on-rushing German infantry, intent on mopping up after the bombers' pounding.'

By 24 April thousands of Allied troops were beginning to gather at the six designated evacuation points on Greece's southern shores. Operation *Demon* – the official evacuation – was to begin that night. But the Luftwaffe had beaten them to it. For over 72 hours *Luftflotte* 4 had been scouring these very waters, attacking anything afloat. On 22 April Stukas had accounted for two 1389-ton Greek destroyers – the *Ydra* as she was leaving Piraeus (Greece's main naval base, where 23 vessels were to be sunk by air attack in just two days!) and the *Psara*, which was at anchor off Megara (one of the evac-

uation beaches). Other Ju 87s of I./StG 2 attacked and sank a number of Greek merchantmen in the Gulf of Corinth. The following day its Stukas had struck further afield, raiding Suda Bay in Crete, while a Sunderland flying-boat evacuating key personnel from Greece was strafed and sunk at its moorings in Scaramanga Bay by seven Ju 87s.

On 24 April troops already arrived at Nauplia – another of the evacuation points – witnessed the destruction of three large freighters by yet more Stukas. Two days later, at the height of *Demon*, Ju 87s attacked a three-ship convoy inbound from Egypt as it entered the Gulf Of Nauplia. Two of the transports were damaged, one so severely that she was immediately towed back to Crete by a destroyer escort. After loading troops overnight, the other was caught by Stukas three hours out of Nauplia early the following morning – the 11,636-ton Dutchman *Slamat* was one of the largest vessels lost during the evacuation.

The Luftwaffe made one last attempt to disrupt British withdrawal plans by mounting a combined glider-borne and paratroop attack on the vital bridge spanning the Corinth Canal. This was the only crossing-point linking mainland Greece to the Peloponnese, where the the three westernmost evacuation beaches were located. Consequently, it was ringed by anti-aircraft defences. The whole region was also packed with columns of Allied troops making their way in unbroken procession towards and across this single artery to safety. Before the six gliders carrying the 54 para-engineers were sent in at dawn on 26 April to seize both ends of the bridge, a force of some 20-30 Stukas attacked the gun positions. They silenced every one of them, while their escorting Bf 110s strafed the immediate area, clearing it for the gliders and follow-up parachute drop.

Despite the qualified success of this daring operation – a massive explosion had destroyed the bridge some ten minutes after the engineers had landed (its exact cause was never established), thus preventing not only further Allied retreat, but also any possibility of rapid German pursuit – the evacuation continued apace. It was completed just after midnight on

Ju 87Rs of II./StG 1 line the perimeter of Argos airfield as they prepare for the invasion of Crete. Note the wreckage of the RAF Hurricane dumped in the dry riverbed in the foreground

30 April, with some three-quarters of the 60,000 troops who had landed in Greece having been lifted off. There *had* been a second Dunkirk after all . . . even down to the masses of vehicles and equipment left behind!

CRETE

The island of Crete, approximately 100 kms from the southernmost tip of the Greek mainland, had already suffered aerial bombardment. Its main anchorage, Suda Bay on the north coast, had been used as a staging point by many of the vessels engaged in the recent evacuation. Having been the spot where British troops first set foot on Greek soil in response to the country's plea for assistance at the time of the original Italian invasion, Crete now represented the last remaining portion of unconquered Greek territory.

Although a pro-Axis government had been installed in Athens on 1 May, the Balkan campaign did not officially 'conclude' until nine days later with the occupation of all of Greece's many minor offshore islands, the Italians taking over those in the Ionian Sea and the Germans occupying those in the Aegean.

The proposal that Crete, too, should be captured – and by airborne invasion – emanated from Generalleutnant Kurt Student, C-in-C XI.*Fliegerkorps*, who controlled all Luftwaffe paratroop and glider forces. The idea was passed quickly up the chain of command, via *Luftflotte* 4 and Göring, to the Führer himself. Mindful of the threat, as he saw it, posed by Crete as a possible base for Allied long-range bombing raids against oil targets in Rumania, and intrigued by the thought of adding an extra dimension to the *Blitzkrieg* concept by taking an island from the air – the first time such an enterprise would have been attempted – Hitler gave the go-ahead, but only if Student could plan to a very tight schedule, as the invasion of the Soviet Union was now little more than a month away.

The story of the invasion itself belongs, quite rightly, to Student's glider-borne and parachute troops, and to the crews of the Ju 52 transports who carried them into battle. They paid the price. But the *Stukagruppen* also had a part to play in Operation *Merkur*, over both the island and, more importantly, the seas surrounding it.

While new airfields were being levelled out of the bare earth of Attica north and west of Athens to house the 500+ Ju 52s and 72 DFS 230 gliders being gathered together for the assault force, the seven *Stukagruppen* of the recent Balkan conflict took up residence further south in the Peloponnese. The majority of them – all three *Gruppen* of StG 77, together with I./StG 1 and I./StG 3 – were concentrated at Argos. Most of I. and III./StG 2 were at first dispersed around Molaoi, but on 14 May Hauptmann Heinrich Brücker led ten selected crews of his III. *Gruppe* out on to the island of Scarpanto (Karpathos), some 80 kms to the east of Crete. From here

Also at Argos, I./StG 3's Ju 87Bs (note the one on the left with a badly-holed rudder) await bombing-up from stocks just delivered

they would be ideally situated to attack shipping along the sealanes between Crete and the British supply bases in Egypt.

In the days leading up to the invasion, the *Stukagruppen* increased their raids along Crete's northern coastline; paying particular attention to the island's three landing grounds and to Suda Bay. It was at Suda on 18 May, for example, that Ju 87s of Hauptmann Hitschhold's I./StG 2 damaged the 15,220-ton Royal Fleet Auxiliary oiler *Olna* so badly that her crew was forced to beach her to prevent her from sinking.

Argos was right on the Peleponese coast. The Stuka landing in the background seems almost out of place in this picture-postcard view of a Greek caique, or sailing vessel, and an Italian CANT air-sea rescue floatplane at rest in the bay

Meanwhile at Molaoi, Oskar Dinort, with the help of I. Gruppe's Technical Officer, was busy improvising a new weapon for use against troops on the ground. The *Geschwaderkommodore* of StG 2 felt that much of the good work done by his pilots in Greece had been dissipated by their bombs burying themselves too deep in the earth before exploding (tell that to the ANZACs!). If a means could be devised for the bombs to be detonated *above* the stony soil of Crete, the scatter effect would be increased enormously.

The obvious solution seemed to be some sort of extension fitted to the nose of the bomb which would cause it to explode before it buried itself. Using a white sheet pegged out in a field of standing crops as a target, the first trials employed 60 cm-long willow sticks screwed into the noses of 50-kg underwing bombs. These proved useless, snapping off and failing to detonate the bombs before impact. The willow sticks were then replaced by metal rods, but these became too easily embedded in the ground and the bombs still exploded a fraction too late.

The third version was successful. With an 8 cm diameter metal disc welded to the end of the rod, the bomb detonated some 30 cm above ground level. Judged by the shallowness of the crater left in the field, and the damage to the crops for a large area around, the effect would be devastating. The first rods were fabricated in the *Geschwader*'s own workshops and were nicknamed 'Dinort's asparagus'. Later manufactured industrially, 'Dinorstäbe' (Dinort's rods) would be widely used throughout the *Stukawaffe*.

The Cretan coastline provided all the visual markers needed for attacking Ju 87 crews seeking out Allied targets. In this shot, a *Kette* of I./StG 77 machines is seen patrolling the northern coast

Operation *Merkur* got under way in the pre-dawn darkness of 20 May as the airborne troops began to climb into the transports. The two weeks of softening-up attacks by the Stukas along the north coast of the island reached their climax in a final series of strikes against the four designated landing and dropping zones shortly after 07.00 hours that morning. These raids, timed to the minute, were designed to keep the

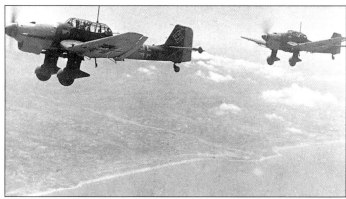

defenders' heads down and prevent them from interfering with the waves of unarmed Ju 52s following immediately behind.

But Student's planners had overlooked one small, but vital, fact. As the first of the transports gathered speed across their newly-prepared airstrips, each left an enormous dust-storm in its wake. The pilots of the following aircraft were completely blinded. Take-off was impossible. Valuable minutes were wasted as successive machines were forced to wait until the dust thrown up by the one in front had settled.

It has been claimed that this involuntary lapse between the Stukas' bombing and the eventual arrival of the transports gave the defenders time to recover and, being fully alerted, inflict heavy casualties on the airborne invaders. In fact, in many instances the opposite was the case. The troops on Crete had grown so accustomed to the daily 'hate' – as they called the morning raids – that they thought the 20 May attacks, albeit slightly earlier than usual, were just more of the same. As soon as the Stukas had disappeared back out to sea, they stood down and began to move to the breakfasts which had been cooking during the raids – many of those at Maleme (the key target in the invasion) not even bothering to take their rifles with them! The 'angry throb' of heavy engines just before 08.00 hours came as a nasty shock, but they recovered quickly, and the punishment they then meted out was to cost the élite 'paras' dear.

In the opening stages of the 12-day conquest of Crete, the Ju 87s were employed for much of the time in their classic role as 'flying artillery', being called upon to bomb into submission particularly stubborn nests of Allied resistance. But they continued to attack more strategic targets, too. On 22 May, for example, they were back over the Suda Bay area. Although only one machine – of StG 77 – failed to return from this particular raid, StG 3 had already lost three aircraft in a disastrous take-off accident at overcrowded Argos beforehand.

Forty-eight hours later Stukas attacked the defenders of Kastelli Bay at the far western end of the island, where a follow-up seaborne force of the 5. *Panzerdivision* was attempting to land light tanks. During the afternoon of that same 24 May, the Cretan capital Canea was dive-bombed 'in relentless rotation', according to one eye-witness. Four Ju 87s of StG 1 were reported missing at the end of this day's operations.

Despite their initial losses, Student's paratroops gradually gained control of the flat coastal belt along the north of the island. The defenders were forced into another hazardous retreat, this time across Crete's mountainous spine to the evacuation beaches on its wilder southern shores. Devoid of air cover (the nearest RAF base was in Egypt), the columns winding their way through the boulder-strewn mountain passes suffered grievously at the hands of strafing Luftwaffe fighters and dive-bombers, the latter now armed with Dinort's deadly 'asparagus';

'We began to dread the Stukas.

A bomb bursts among shipping anchored in Suda Bay – one large vessel is already burning fiercely from a direct hit

At the slightest movement, the ugly, bent-winged Junkers circled the spot with their oil stained bellies turned towards us. One by one, in leisurely fashion, they peeled off, screaming down in a vertical dive, airbrakes extended, sirens wailing, to release their bombs with deadly accuracy. Within minutes the chosen area would be plastered with high-explosives.'

Somebody else caught in the mountains – more stoical, or perhaps simply better hidden among the rocks – recalled;

'. . . one particular aircraft that I could recognise from a smudge near the cross on its starboard wing must have remained overhead for more than an hour, buzzing backwards and forwards, round and round, until I was heartily sick of it.'

Devastating though the dive-bomber raids on the island undoubtedly were, it was in the seas surrounding Crete that the Stukas made their greatest impact. The Royal Navy was very active in the area. Adm Cunningham initially had three 'light task forces' – mixed groups of cruisers and destroyers – sweeping the Aegean during the hours of darkness. But mindful of his ships' vulnerability to enemy air attack from mainland Greece and other island bases, these vessels were ordered to withdraw at dawn to less dangerous waters south of Crete. To do so they had the choice of two routes – either to the west or the east of the embattled island.

The Stukas' first victim, the destroyer *Juno*, had successfully negotiated the eastern route (the Kaso Strait between Crete and Scarpanto) and was some 80 kms beyond when she was caught just after midday on 21 May by Ju 87s of Hauptmann Brücker's Scarpanto-based III./StG 2 and bombers of the Regia Aeronautica. *Juno* was hit by three bombs, one of which detonated her main magazine. Broken in two by the resulting explosions, she sank in two minutes with heavy loss of life. Just before dusk, action switched to the western end of Crete where another force of three cruisers and four destroyers was entering the Antikythera Channel preparatory to a sweep along the island's northern coast. Attacked by other elements of III./StG 2 from the Peloponnese, this force suffered no damage but claimed two Ju 87s – one broken completely in half by a direct AA hit, and the second ditching before it could reach land.

The following morning Royal Navy units attempting to leave the

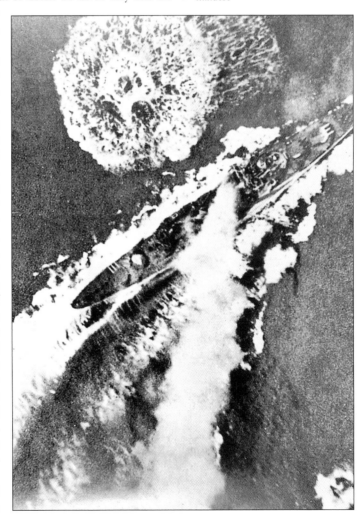

Near misses straddle the cruiser *Gloucester* moments before a succession of direct hits brought her to a standstill. She subsequently keeled over and sank in a matter of minutes

area via this same western route came under heavy air attack. They called for assistance from a Battle Squadron which was on station to the west of Crete. Answering the call, the latter itself became the target for Stuka attack in the early afternoon. The heavily-armoured battleship *Warspite* 'shrugged off' a single hit from a Ju 87, while other aircraft of I. and III./StG 2 damaged the cruisers *Gloucester* and *Fiji*, again not seriously. But the destroyer *Greyhound* was struck by three bombs just before 14.00 hours and went down in minutes. Standing by to cover the rescue of survivors, the two cruisers were again set upon by a mixed formation of Ju 87s and Ju 88s. Singled out by Oberleutnant Dr Ernst Kupfer's 3./StG 1, the 9400-ton *Gloucester* was hit repeatedly and brought to a standstill, badly on fire. The ship which had survived attack by II./StG 2 off Malta in January was not to escape a second time. Within minutes she too had gone under (retiring southwards still under heavy air attack, the *Fiji* was sunk soon afterwards by Bf 109 fighter-bombers).

As darkness fell three destroyers from Malta, under the command of Capt Lord Louis Mountbatten in *Kelly*, passed through the Antikythera Channel with orders to bombard Maleme airfield. They exited by the same route in the early hours of the next morning. Daybreak on 23 May found them well south of Crete, but not yet out of Stuka range. At 07.55 hours they were spotted by more than 20 Ju 87s of I./StG 2, led by *Gruppenkommandeur* Hauptmann Hubertus Hitschhold. The dive-bombers attacked immediately. After taking a hit amidships, *Kashmir* sank in less than two minutes. Despite violent evasive manoeuvres, *Kelly* could not escape the same fate, a bomb striking her in the engine room and causing her to capsize almost at once – half the ship's company went down with the destroyer. The third vessel, *Kipling*, picked up 279 survivors from her two sisters.

Forty-eight hours later the action reverted to Crete's eastern extremities. The Royal Navy had known of the presence of Stukas on Scarpanto from the beginning. Three destroyers had bombarded the island early on the morning of 21 May, but now Hauptmann Brücker's original ten crews had been reinforced by the remainder of III. *Gruppe*, plus those of I./StG 2. It was to neutralise this perceived threat to shipping in the eastern Mediterranean (and in particular to the evacuation that now appeared increasingly likely) that another Battle Squadron sailed from Alexandria on 25 May. Comprising the battleships *Queen Elizabeth* and *Barham*, the carrier *Formidable* and an escort of nine destroyers, the Squadron's air strike against Scarpanto at dawn on 26 May did little material damage. Withdrawing at speed, the ships braced themselves for inevitable reprisal. It came in the early afternoon, when the Squadron was already some 250 kms south of Kaso Strait. It also

The destroyers *Kelly*, *Kashmir* and *Kipling* attempt to escape the hail of bombs dropped by I./StG 2 Stukas. *Kashmir* has already disappeared beneath a forest of explosions (centre left), and *Kelly* would soon meet the same fate

came from a most unexpected direction – North Africa.

Uninvolved in the Cretan operations, Major Walter Enneccerus and his 20 Stukas of II./StG 2 were not even searching for the Battle Squadron. They were hunting supply ships making for Tobruk, and were almost at the limit of their range when they sighted the outer screen of destroyers. The *Gruppenkommandeur* immediately led his three *Staffeln* in an attack against the prime target – the carrier. Although he did not inflict as much damage on the *Formidable* as he had on her sister ship, the *Illustrious*, off Malta at the beginning of the year, the two direct hits scored on her flightdeck, together with several near misses, were sufficient to put her out of action for over a year.

Solar-topeed Stuka crews tour the wreckage of the 9600-ton cruiser *York* in Suda Bay after the capture of Crete. Although she had drawn dive-bomber attacks like a magnet, the *York* had, in fact, been torpedoed by an Italian 'one-man torpedo boat' two months earlier, and had been resting on the bottom of the bay throughout the campaign

One of the destroyer escorts had her bow blown off by another bomb – the *Nubian*, too, would spend the next twelve months undergoing extensive repair.

But it was another 'light task force', departing Alexandria on 28 May, which was to provide the Stukas with their last sinking of the campaign. Bound for Heraklion to evacuate one of the few remaining pockets of organised resistance on Crete's northern coastline, the three cruisers and six destroyers were subjected to ten separate air attacks on the way. Although no ships were hit, a cruiser and a destroyer both suffered near misses, the former being ordered back to Alexandria, while the latter continuing on to Heraklion, where it was abandoned and sunk the next morning after developing catastrophic steering gear failure.

It was shortly after she went down that the seven surviving vessels, crammed with troops and just about to enter Kaso Strait, were attacked by the first wave of Stukas from nearby Scarpanto. A single bomb from a III./StG 2 machine struck the 1300-ton *Hereward* near her forward funnel. The destroyer reduced speed and swung out of formation, making for the coast of Crete which was only some seven kilometres away. Before she could reach it she took further hits and sank. Most of the crew and the 450 soldiers aboard were rescued to become prisoners-of-war.

Although the *Hereward* was the sixth and last victim to succumb to dive-bomber attack off Crete, the Stukas still had one parting shot. Elements of StG 77 and I./StG 3 chased after the depleted 'light task force' and severely damaged both cruisers *Dido* and *Orion*, before they finally passed out of range.

Three days later the *Stukagruppen* had turned their backs on the Mediterranean and were heading north. It was June 1941, and Hitler could at long last concentrate on more important business – the invasion of the Soviet Union.

CAMPAIGNS IN NORTH AFRICA

Whilst the conflict in the Balkans and the eastern Mediterranean was rapidly nearing a satisfactory conclusion for the Axis alliance thanks in no small part to the efforts of the *Stukageschwader*, the three Ju 87 units which had left Sicily back in late January and flown south across the Mediterranean to Tripoli, in North Africa, had been fighting a very different kind of war. Granted, the common enemy may not have changed, but conditions certainly had.

As Libya was then part of the Italian Empire, the personnel of 96° *Gruppo* adapted to their new surroundings fairly quickly. But for the crews of I./StG 1 and II./StG 2 (the majority of whom had been recruited in north Germany), everything was new. There was a lot to be learned. From a personal level (never put your boots on in the morning without first checking them for scorpions!) to operating procedures (do not inflate an aircraft's tyres to the correct pressure at the beginning of the day, as by noon, the sun's heat will likely cause them to burst – in respect to the latter point, the Germans later discovered that their Buna artificial compound was better able to withstand the rigours of desert campaigning than natural rubber). They even had to turn to

The new arrivals had to learn to cope with the all-pervading desert sand

Members of the newly-arrived *Afrika Korps* watch a *Ketten* of Stukas roar low overhead . . .

. . . while others get an even closer look. A machine of I./StG 1 is seen here being given the once-over on a landing strip alongside a typical desert oasis of waving palms

But picturesque scenery meant little to those unsung heroes of the North African campaign – the ground-crews. Here, a mechanic carries out a last-minute check on the engine of a Stuka bombed-up and ready to go

the Italians for suitable lubricants, as the grease they normally used on moving metal parts simply melted and drained away, resulting in seized engines and jammed weapons.

So much to assimilate, and so little time to do it in, for the Stukas' presence in Africa was yet another example of Hitler's stepping in to aid his southern ally. At the start of the Mediterranean war, on 10 June 1940, Italian and British troops were facing each other across the wire of the Libyan-Egyptian border. It was the Italians who finally made the first move, Marshal Graziani's forces descending the Halfaya Pass into Egypt on 13 September. They moved forward some 100 kms to Sidi Barrani, where they dug in and stayed put.

On 9 December Gen Wavell counter-attacked. This first British offensive not only drove the numerically superior Italians out of Egypt, it pushed them right back across Cyrenaica (Libya's eastern province) and saw Bardia, Tobruk and Benghazi (the provincial capital) captured along the way. For the Italians it was Albania and Greece all over again.

By the first week of February 1941, having advanced over 800 kms, Wavell's troops came to a halt at El Agheila. In the North African campaign, geography – in the form of impassable inland sand seas – dictated that all major operations had to be conducted along the relatively narrow

Without mechanical aids, the fitting of an underwing fuel tank was a many-handed job

41

4./StG 2 sets out across Cyrenaica. Just visible on their starboard cowlings . . .

. . . is the badge adopted by the *Staffel* shortly after their arrival in North Africa

coastal belt bordering the Mediterranean. Another immutable law was that as one side advanced, and its lines of communications and supply lengthened, it would gradually grow weaker, whereas the enemy, being forced back ever closer to his own rear-area supply bases, gathered strength until, like a coiled spring, he in his turn was able to unleash a counter-offensive.

The war in North Africa would see-saw back and forth no fewer than six times before the final outcome. Graziani's initial push eastwards into Egypt, and Wavell's answering westward thrust deep into Libya, were but the first two swings of the pendulum. And it was at this juncture that Wavell's already somewhat precarious position (he had long outrun his land communications and was having to rely on units of the Mediterranean Fleet's Inshore Squadron to bring up supplies by sea) was made worse by two outside factors – the withdrawal of British desert troops being sent to the aid of Greece, and the arrival in North Africa of German forces coming to the assistance of the Italians.

As the sole offensive weaponry available to the embryonic *'Fliegerführer Afrika'*, the 60 Ju 87s of I./StG 1 and II./StG 2 were flung into the fray almost immediately. Their task was twofold – to soften up the enemy prior to the imminent German counter-offensive, and to prevent his supplies getting through by bombing the ports along the Cyrenaican coast now held by the British.

I./StG 1 was to suffer the first Stuka loss of the African campaign when one of its machines was brought down by anti-aircraft fire over El Agheila on 14 February. Four days later, and further along the coast near Mersa Brega, the same *Gruppe* was also the first to encounter aerial opposition – 12 of its Ju 87s were attacked by Hurricanes, who claimed the destruction of eight of the dive-bombers.

On 22 February a Stuka raid on Benghazi damaged the coastal monitor *Terror*. The vessel was sunk two days later while trying to reach Alexandria. In the meantime the Ju 87s had sent the 1375-ton destroyer *Dainty* to the bottom – or 'trodden her under water', to use the Stuka crews' own vernacular for a sinking. Land targets were also dive-bombed with increasing intensity until, on 31 March, the Germans launched their counter-attack. Initially intended simply to be a 'reconnaissance-in-force', the German commander – one Generalleutnant Erwin Rommel – quickly recognised and exploited his enemy's weakness.

The 'reconnaissance' soon became a full-blown offensive, and in little over a month all Libya was back in Axis hands, with German troops just inside the Egyptian border occupying the rocky escarpment of the Halfaya Pass. Inevitably dubbed 'Hellfire Pass' by Allied troops, this bottleneck on the strategically vital road between the two countries became the scene of much fierce fighting.

To say *all* Libya was back in Axis hands is not strictly accurate. True,

In those early months in the desert the Bf 109-escorted Stuka was a for-midable weapon indeed. Here, another 4. *Staffel* Ju 87B-2 trop enjoys the protection offered by Oberleutnant Ludwig Franzisket, *Gruppen-Adjutant* of I./StG 27

But there were losses too. Here, a Ju 87 has crashed (top left) on to a small bluff right next to the Via Balbia, the *Afrika Korps*' main sup-ply route. A soldier hurries to the rescue

Two main types of mission were carried out by the Stukas during the spring of 1941 – against the enemy's ground forces (this 4./StG 2 machine is seen chasing its shadow across the desert still wears its orig-inal clover-leaf badge) . . .

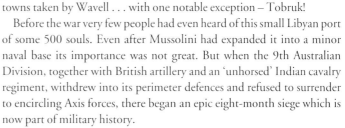

Rommel had restored all the territory lost by the Italians at the turn of the year, and in his advance eastwards, he had also re-occupied all the coastal towns taken by Wavell . . . with one notable exception – Tobruk!

Before the war very few people had even heard of this small Libyan port of some 500 souls. Even after Mussolini had expanded it into a minor naval base its importance was not great. But when the 9th Australian Division, together with British artillery and an 'unhorsed' Indian cavalry regiment, withdrew into its perimeter defences and refused to surrender to encircling Axis forces, there began an epic eight-month siege which is now part of military history.

Throughout those eight months Rommel tried time and again to elim-inate this threat to his immediate rear (Tobruk was only some 150 kms behind his frontline troops astride the Egyptian frontier). Its continued occupation by the enemy also denied him its use as a forward supply port. For the Allies, it was equally essential that Tobruk should hold out for as long as possible. By tying up a significant number of Rommel's forces, and by hindering his build-up of supplies, the garrison's presence was not only preventing him from advancing any further towards his declared objective, Alexandria, it was also buying valuable time for the British Army in Egypt to make good its recent losses and prepare for its own imminent counter-offensive.

... and against British coastal shipping. This aircraft, (from the same *Staffel* as the Ju 87 seen on the previous page) is seen returning low overwater, clearly wearing the new palm tree emblem on its distinctive nose cowling

Tobruk, and its environment, were to dominate Stuka operations in the western desert for much of the remainder of the year. The port installations and the town itself were bombed repeatedly, as too were the landward defences originally constructed by the Italians – the 45 kms of outer perimeter wire and fortifications, the blockhouses, the inner wire, the seven forts and two landing grounds.

The harbour became littered with sunken ships, whilst the route along the coast from Alexandria to Tobruk used by transports and vessels of the Inshore Squadron to ferry supplies to the beleaguered garrison was soon known to all as 'Bomb Alley'.

Just as the Stukas were beginning their costly eight-month duel with the defenders of Tobruk, some organisational changes took place. On the very day that the Axis ring closed around the town, the long-range Ju 87Rs of 7. and 8./StG 1 departed Trapani, on Sicily, for Tripoli. They were soon to replace

Allied shipping is seen under attack in Tobruk harbour from the viewpoint of a marauding Ju 87 crew ...

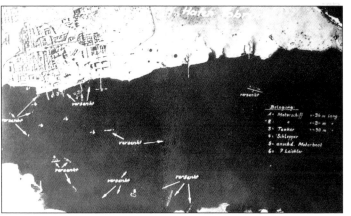

... and an official photo-recce shot analyses the *Staffel*'s results, detailing the ships present and arrows pointing to those that were sunk

Major Hozzel's I./StG 1, which was being withdrawn from Libya to take part in Operation *Marita.*

In view of their maritime background (III./StG 1 had originally been activated for service aboard the never-to-be-completed aircraft carrier *Graf Zeppelin*), it appears that the *Staffeln's* services were called upon whenever a shipping target presented itself. After transferring forward to Derna to join Major Enneccerus' II./StG 2 (who only the day before had carpet-bombed Tobruk's outer defences in support of the opening land assault on the garrison), 7. and 8./StG 1's first operation – on 12 April – was against an inbound supply ship still some distance out to sea. It was not altogether successful.

Although the unidentified vessel was reportedly hit, it succeeded in bringing down one of its attackers. According to another crew, who saw the 7. *Staffel* machine crash into the sea a few hundred metres astern of the target, the ship had fired some sort of parachute rocket dragging a length of wire behind it! Furthermore, visibility, which had not been good at take-off, had degenerated into a raging sandstorm by the time the Stukas returned to Derna. Two aircraft were forced to land early; one behind enemy lines. The sandstorm did not blow itself out until the afternoon of the following day.

Despite having been in Africa for less than a week, the newcomers had already been introduced to one of the local delicacies – tinned Australian fruit from captured enemy stocks. Having consumed the contents while waiting for the storm to abate (or 'for the desert to land', as one wag put it), the tins came in very handy to scoop the sand out of

A *Kette* of III./StG 1 flies back over the coast on its return flight to Derna after completing an early attack on Tobruk in April 1941

One picture is worth a thousand words, and this one says it all – the crew of this Stuka relax in deck-chairs in the shade of the starboard wing as they await their next mission. The aircraft is bombed up for another raid on Tobruk, but long-range fuel tanks are also ready should there be a last-minute change in the target necessitating a lengthy overwater sortie. Meanwhile, the tyres are protected against the growing heat of the day – and note the light paintwork on the rear part of the undercarriage leg and spat (see colour profile five)

This Stuka (top) pounds Fort Pilastrino, one of the main fortifications inside Tobruk's inner ring of defences

their untropicalised machines. It was a relatively easy job to empty the cockpits, but the pilots swore for weeks afterwards that they could hear the grinding of their gearboxes!

After a mission against Fort Solario (part of Tobruk's inner defences) on 17 April, Hauptmann Helmut Mahlke of III./StG 1 received orders direct from the 'Fliegerführer Afrika' early next morning to attack a 'battleship' reported by the army to be shelling its forward positions near the Hal-faya Pass. Leading a dozen of his Stukas, Mahlke found the vessel steaming at high speed towards the Gulf of Sollum. It certainly had the broad-beamed outline of a capital ship – 'like a flatiron ploughing through the sea' – and Mahlke ordered his crews into battle formation. It was not until he was committed to his dive that the *Kommandeur* began to have doubts. As the target grew larger in his sights, he could make out more detail. There appeared to be a circular track enclosing a single turret on both the fore- and afterdecks. No more time for speculation. At an altitude of 300 metres Mahlke released his 500-kg bomb.

It was a classic Stuka attack – all nine aircraft of the first three *Ketten* reported hits or near misses. The fourth Kette could no longer see the ship and brought their bombs back home. Mahlke's report to the 'Fliegerführer Afrika' read, in part

'11.05 hours warship or armed merchantman of approx 8000 BRT, probably old coastal monitor, sunk in sea area NE of Sollum. Own losses nil.'

The identity of III./StG 1's 'victim' remains a mystery, however, for the elderly 7200-ton monitor *Terror* had already gone down off Derna nearly two months earlier. Besides, she only had a single, two-gun, turret. The most likely candidate would appear to be one of the several small, twin-turret river gunboats active in this very area at the time, although none of these were lost on this date. But whoever she was and whatever her fate, the army's 'battleship' seems, in all likelihood, to have been a 625-ton vessel the size of a larger trawler!

More attacks by both *Gruppen* on the Tobruk perimeter followed. In the course of these the senior *Kommandeur*, Major Enneccerus, 'suggested' that as Mahlke deployed only two *Staffeln*, the Picchiatelli of the understrength 96° *Gruppo* should be temporarily attached to fly in his

An early example of German-Italian co-operation over the Western Desert – note the painted out Luftwaffe cross on the port wing of the Italian Ju 87

vacant 9. *Staffel* slot. The first such combined operation did not go quite according to plan, however. After attacking British artillery emplacements Mahlke climbed slowly away, weaving as usual to allow his pilots time to catch up and regain formation. But no sign of the Italians:

'At last, in the light of the already setting sun, far, far to the west and at very high altitude, I spotted a few tiny little specks: our Picchiatelli! But they couldn't possibly be in that position if they had followed us down to the bomb release height of 500 metres as ordered. They had probably bombed from 2000 metres and then cleared off out of it. That wouldn't do at all!'

Mahlke gave explicit instructions for the next mission;

'Order of attack: Stab – 7. *Staffel* – Picchiatelli – 8. *Staffel*. Bomb release height 300 metres. Retire northwards over Tobruk at low level. Re-form over open water, turn west once out of flak range.'

Sandwiched between the two German *Staffeln*, the Picchiatelli carried out these orders to the letter. During debriefing at *'Fliegerführer Afrika'* HQ Mahlke awaited an opportunity to congratulate the leader of the Italian formation. He did not get the chance. The latter came rushing up, gesticulating wildly. The interpreter could hardly keep up with the excited torrent of words; 'That was fantastic! This time we could see our target quite clearly and actually hit it! Now at last we know how it's done. Nobody's ever told us or shown us properly before!' It would appear that training procedures had declined somewhat since those first two courses at Graz-Thalerhof.

By the end of April the last fighters stationed within the Tobruk perimeter had been withdrawn to Egypt. Henceforth the garrison's defence would be dependent upon its own anti-aircraft artillery, which at this stage consisted of 88 pieces – 28 heavy (90 mm and above), 17 40 mm Bofors and the remainder captured Italian 20 mm Bredas. Fortunately,

early in May the defenders noticed a slight easing of Axis pressure, both on the ground and in the air. This coincided with III./StG 1's return to Trapani, and thence to Greece for participation in the Cretan campaign. Their place was taken temporarily by II./StG 1, who would remain in Africa for less than three weeks to bridge the gap until the return of I./StG 1 from the Balkans.

The first *Staffel* to arrive in the desert was 3./StG 1 on 19 May, the rest of the *Gruppe* not rejoining until the following month after their short sojourn in Sardinia. In the mean-time, a dive-bombing attack on Tobruk harbour on 12 May – pre-sumably by II./StG 2 – had caught one of the little gunboats. Although she was now resting on the bottom, the decks of the *Ladybird* were just above water, and gunners would continue to man the dual-purpose 3-inch gun under her bridge and her foremost pom-poms – a useful addi-tion to the port's immediate defences.

The cessation of hostilities in Albania and mainland Greece had,

The Stuka was a remarkably versa-tile aircraft. It could provide a wind-break while getting dressed . . .

. . . act as a shelf for stowing tackle and other toiletries . . .

. . . and even cater for more basic functions. And no, this is not a Ju 87*P*!

The *Gruppenkommandeur* of I./StG 3 gets set to roll. Note the fighter-style command chevrons ahead of the fuselage code

Above and right
Two fully bombed-up Stukas provide an interesting contrast in camouflage. With a cluster of eight fragmentation bombs beneath each wing, 'HK' boasts a tan scheme overall. Carrying the more usual four 50 kg underwing bombs, the second Ju 87 has received an irregular dapple finish but, as yet, no unit marking (but note the Wk-Nr just discernable at the top of the rudder)

however, released two other dive-bomber units for service elsewhere. While the Italian 101° *Gruppo* retired from Albania to Gerbini in Sicily, from where they would mount intermittent night attacks against Malta for the remainder of the year, the Picchiatelli of 97° *Gruppo* departed Lecce, on the heel of Italy, and crossed the Mediterranean for North Africa.

The latter were soon putting to good use the 'ship-busting' tactics they had perfected in the waters around Corfu. On 25 May they sank the 3741-ton tanker *Helka*, which was en route from Alexandria with a cargo of petroleum for the Tobruk garrison. They also damaged her escorting sloop, the 990-ton *Grimsby*, which went down after subsequent attacks by Ju 87s of 3./StG 1. In mid-June the Picchi-

Meanwhile, II./StG 2s European-green Ju 87B-2 trops continued to shuttle back and forth to Tobruk – with a coastline like that to follow, who needs maps

atelli were called upon to help the Stukas of I./StG 1 and II.StG 2 repulse a second British attempt to relieve Tobruk overland from Egypt, after which they turned their attention back to the Inshore Squadron, and its efforts to keep the beleaguered garrison supplied by sea.

The story of these supply runs is a saga in itself. They had begun almost from the moment Tobruk was surrounded. But early attempts to send in merchantmen during daylight hours had soon shown how hazardous – if not impossible – it would be to maintain supplies in this way. The convoy service ships *Fiona* and *Chakla*, sunk by dive-bombers in April, were but two of many. The task of replacing them fell on the hard-pressed Mediterranean destroyers, who began a regular night service – known as the 'Spud Run' – between Alexandria and Tobruk. But even they were at risk on clear, moonlit, nights.

Five days after the loss of the sloop *Auckland*, dive-bombed off Tobruk on 24 June, it was the long wakes being trailed in the dusk sea off Sollum by the destroyers *Waterhen* and *Defender* which betrayed their presence to seven Picchiatelli of 239ª *Squadriglia*. At the head of the seven was Giuseppe Cenni, who immediately adopted his usual low-level 'method' of attack, scoring direct hits amidships on the lead destroyer. Although the Australian-crewed *Waterhen* did not sink at once, she capsized in the early hours of the following morning.

Shortly afterwards the 'poachers' turned 'gamekeepers' when 239ª was withdrawn to Benghazi for rest and refit. Here, they were employed on convoy protection and anti-submarine patrols along the Axis' own supply sealanes off the coast of Cyrenaica. On 30 July they surprised HM submarine *Cachalot* on the surface and damaged her so badly that she was unable to submerge; later being rammed and sunk by an Italian destroyer.

To augment the destroyers on the 'Spud Run', the Navy even dispatched their slow and cumbersome 'A' and 'D' lighters to Tobruk. These early landing craft (better known under their later wartime designations as LCTs and LCMs) also suffered at the hands of the dive-bombers. Then

there was the fleet of small trawlers, schooners and luggers which would aim to arrive at Tobruk just before dawn, unload during the day hidden alongside one or another of the many wrecks in the harbour, and leave again at dark.

One of the most famous of these was the 400-ton schooner *Maria Giovanna*, captured from the Italians and now skippered by an Australian RNR Lt named Alfred Palmer, but known to one and all as 'Pedlar'. It was 'Pedlar's' proud boast that he could navigate to Tobruk by the headlights of enemy convoys along the coast road, but even he admitted to a sense of relief every time the dim green lights marking the entrance to Tobruk harbour hove into view. 'Pedlar's career was finally brought to an end not by Stukas, but by much more underhand means. The enemy sneakily planted a second green light just before Tobruk and he ran aground. The story has it that when troops waded out to capture him, 'Pedlar' and his entire crew were up to their necks in water frantically digging a channel to get the *Maria Giovanna* back out into open water!

Top and above
Tobruk's waterfront takes another battering from Stukas screaming down from high overhead

While all this was going on, II./StG 2 and the newly-returned I./StG 1 were keeping up the pressure on Tobruk's perimeter defences. As there were now no fighters based in the immediate area, it was often a straight contest between the dive-bombers and the anti-aircraft defences. Although not of the same frequency and ferocity as the almost daily attacks flown during the early weeks of the siege, these raids still exacted a steady toll among the Stuka crews. For not only were more guns being delivered to the garrison almost by the day, but the gunners were also refining their tactics.

Instead of concentrating a box barrage at a specific height above the harbour area, for example, the defenders 'thickened the belt' by altering the ceiling and spreading the pattern over an altitude of 1000 metres or more, thus forcing the Ju 87s to brave the barrage for a much longer period during their dives. And to counter the Stukas' trick of coming down along the edge of the barrage and then sliding under it, the gunners

Two of the mediterranean greats –
Major Walter Ennecerus, who led
II./StG 2 (latterly III./StG 3) throughout almost the entire desert campaign . . .

. . . and Major Walter Sigel,
Kommandeur of I./StG 3, who was
promoted to *Kommodore* of StG 3
for the last 12 months of the
Geschwader's service in North
Africa

also directed their fire from side to side. A pilot might start his dive clear of the barrage and then find it had swung into his line of flight. Perversely, many Stuka crews took these 'improvements' to be a sign of the enemy's weakening; 'Defensive fire is no longer so well-disciplined and much more ragged at the edges'.

Towards the end of August the *Geschwaderstab* StG 3, under Ober-stleutnant Walter Sigel, arrived from Greece to take command of the two desert *Stukagruppen* – I./StG 1 still at Derna and II./StG 2 now at Tmimi, somewhat closer to Tobruk (it was from Tmimi that II./StG 2 had dis-covered and attacked the carrier *Formidable* retiring from Scarpanto back in May). Fortunately, the Kommodore himself was not aboard the Stab Bf 110 which was sent to have a look at the Tobruk defences on 29 August and which failed to return . . . the AA gunners' aim wasn't that ragged!

Stab StG 3 were to lose another aircraft on 14 September when one of their Ju 87s was downed while landing at Gambut, east of Tobruk. But the main dive-bomber occurrence of that day took place further east still, over Egypt, where the 12 Picchiatelli of 209[a] *Squadriglia* had been despatched to cover an Axis recce push towards Sidi Barrani. Losing both their Bf 109 escort and their bearings, ten Ju 87s ran out of fuel and force-landed all over the Western Desert. Eight of the crew fell into British hands and word soon got around that at least one of the aircraft had come down intact somewhere up near the frontier in the Fort Maddalena area.

Two RAF officers got permission to go and look for it and, if possible, fly it back. An aerial search the first day discovered little more than one of the other Stukas lying on its back near Thalata. The next day the pair con-tinued by truck, kindly supplied by a famous Hussar regiment whose guests they had been overnight. This time they had more luck, finding the Junkers, still fully bombed-up, standing on a stretch of firm sand. The young British army officer reclining by its side with a certain air of proud possession was nonetheless quite happy to hand over his charge.

The new owners faced three problems – was the aircraft booby-trapped? – how to remove the bombs? – and how to get it back in the air? – all the instruments and controls were still labelled in the original Ger-man. Problems one and two were solved, respectively, by (a) having a look and (b) pulling the bomb-release lever – the latter not without a moment's anxiety! Number three would only be resolved by trial and error. Pouring in the 12 gallons of aviation spirit they had brought with them, topped up by another 20 of ordinary petrol donated by the ever-helpful Hussars, they soon had the Junkers' engine purring nicely. It was almost dusk as they took off and set course north-eastwards.

After some 15 minutes of steady cruising the engine suddenly stopped without warning and the aircraft floated groundwards. The pilot man-aged to put it down on the rough desert surface with no more damage than a burst tyre. A little tinkering and they were off again. But this flight was even shorter. The hydraulic gauge exploded, the fluid momentarily blinding the pilot. But again he was able to land, this time to the detri-ment of the other tyre!

After a night spent under the Junkers wrapped in an Italian parachute, the pair decided next morning to walk to Sidi Barrani which, they esti-mated, was some 40 miles away. Reluctant to abandon their prize to an uncertain fate, they scratched a message on the ground before setting out;

'This Ju 87 is RAF property. *DO NOT TOUCH.* W/Cdr Bowman and S/Ldr Rozier left here at dawn 19/9/41 walking north.'

Ten miles later they came across a South African officer who invited them back to his camp for breakfast. Here, a new plan was hatched. They would return to the wrecked Junkers at Thalata, retrieve its hydraulic gauge and a spare wheel, and then – with any luck – be on their way again. By this time it seemed as if everybody in the forward area was taking an interest in the two pilots and their Junkers. They were now being accompanied by a Tank Corps officer, who had

Top and above
Two of the Picchiatelli lost during the 14 September disaster which won't be flying again. The crew of Wk-Nr 5794 appear to have set fire to their machine before heading back to Libya on foot. And could the overturned example (note the bomb still in site!) be the Thalata wreck which provided the spares for the one 'flyer' captured by the Allies?

lent them his truck, a couple of RAF technicians, and had even picked up a bearded young Royal Navy destroyer captain, who had been due a spot of leave and was spending it in the Western Desert 'having a look around'!

Everything ran like clockwork. They picked up the spares. The technicians fitted the new gauge, replaced the wheel and revived the engine. And the naval officer, to round off a perfect holiday, asked if he could take the rear gunner's seat for the trip back. There was just one snag. On the way they flew low over several British gun emplacements, whose occupants had not been able to keep up with the rapid sequence of events and to whom every bent-winged, fixed-undercarriage aircraft was an enemy Stuka . . . even if there was a Royal Navy officer hanging out of the back cockpit, face redder than his beard, who was suggesting at the top of his voice that they desist shooting at him in language that was all too clearly neither German nor Italian!

After many trials and tribulations (detailed in the text for this chapter), Wk-Nr 5763 – aircraft '18' – arrived safely at an RAF forward landing ground

Back at a more permanent base, and with a set of the 'new owner's' markings applied, the Picchiatello has become an object of some curiosity

Two months to the day after this episode, British and Commonwealth troops under Gen Auchinleck launched their counter-offensive. Operation *Crusader* – the fourth swing of the pendulum – would recoup all the enemy territory won and then lost again by Wavell at the beginning of the year. In just five weeks Auchinleck would be entering Benghazi, having pushed Rommel back to his jumping-off point at El Agheila.

It was just as *Crusader* was starting that I./StG 3 arrived in Libya from Rhodes. After their relatively peaceful existence in the eastern Mediterranean, the contrast could not have been greater. The opening rounds of *Crusader* witnessed a succession of savage and confused clashes between opposing ground and air forces alike. But with Allied fighter strength now, for the first time, almost on a parity with that of the Axis, the writing was clearly on the wall for the Ju 87. All three *Stukagruppen* began to suffer much heavier losses as enemy fighters tore into them in the air and

Still decked out in dual markings 209a *Squadriglia*'s number '18' is put through her paces. The aircraft was predominantly flown by pilots of No 39 Sqn, based at Ikingi Maryut, in the months immediately after its capture. The Stuka remained in airworthy condition with the RAF (coded HK827) for nearly three years, its last recorded flight taking place at El Ballah, in the Suez Canal Zone, on 27 September 1944. The aircraft was scrapped soon afterwards, however, due to corrosion in the wing structure. The date of this final flight means that Wk-Nr 5763 was almost certainly the last remaining airworthy Ju 87 in North Africa

attacked them on the ground.

On the morning of 20 November (the third day of *Crusader*), six out of a formation of twelve I./StG 1 aircraft were claimed destroyed or damaged. That same afternoon 18 more – many of them II./StG 2 machines at Tmimi – were shot up at their bases. Three days later Ju 87s of Stab and I./StG 3 were being added to the casualty figures. On the last day of the month a further 15 Stukas were either shot down or claimed as probables, and on 4 December another 13 suffered a similar fate. And so it went on. But with every *Gruppe* already well below half strength, for how long could it continue?

Not only were many Stukas prevented from reaching their objectives (forced instead to jettison their bombs early), those that did get through were having less effect on their intended targets. A lot of the troops involved in *Crusader* had been through it all before on the other side of the Mediterranean;

Elsewhere, the war goes on as large formations of Luftwaffe Stukas continue to support the *Afrika Korps'* advance on Egypt

'Now we had a completely different angle on dive-bombers. In Greece and Crete all the talk was of Stukas. Men with no air cover at all were dive-bombed for hours on end in trenches and gun emplacements. In Greece, I remember, there was a theory that it was not worth while firing back at the Stukas because they were armoured against rifle and machine-gun bullets. The result was that they did what they were meant to do – keep the men in the slit-trenches, and therefore out of the battle.

'But in the desert it all looked different. There was space, and if vehicles are properly dispersed, the biggest target a dive-bomber can hope for is something the size of a tank or large lorry, and there will be no subsidiary target for 50 yards around if he misses. It came to be realised that dive-bombing was frightening out of all proportion to its danger. And as soon as that was realised it became less frightening.

'It gave men courage to stand up and fire back at the Stukas, and when they did so they found they could bring them down. I once saw 25 Stukas stage a ten-minute raid and wound one man in the leg. We calculated that leg-wound had cost Hitler all of £50,000.

'There was another point in which Libya differed from Greece and Crete. This time we had air superiority, and the dive-bomber had no chance against a fast fighter. So the Germans began to use their Stukas warily and infrequently. Few people got more than two or three bouts of dive-bombing in the course of the whole campaign.'

On 7 December 1941 the eight-month siege of Tobruk was finally

A casualty of one such operation provides the recipe for some propaganda sleight-of-hand – take one crashed and abandoned Stuka (tail Swastika already removed by souvenir hunters), light a small fire under its nose, add an 'advancing' infantryman, and a bogus British 'counter-attack' is in full swing!

raised. But this day of celebration in the Western Desert will forever be eclipsed in history by the 'Day of Infamy' on the other side of the world as Japan attacked Pearl Harbour. And unlike the defenders of the Metaxas Line, who had held out under Stuka bombardment for three days, the Tobruk garrison received no grudging words of praise from Hitler. But they were quite content with the epithet bestowed on them by Doktor Goebbels' propaganda machine. The 'Rats of Tobruk', they felt, had a certain ring to it.

The relief of Tobruk marked the end of the Stuka's dominance in North Africa. With enemy fighter strength increasing, it was threatening to become the Battle of Britain all over again. But for the three *Stuka-gruppen* currently retreating across Cyrenaica, there was to be no safe cross-Channel haven to which they could retire to lick their wounds. Instead, redesignated and re-equipped, they would continue to fight until the *Afrika Korps* finally laid down its arms – and beyond, for there would be a Stuka presence in the Mediterranean theatre right up until the ultimate surrender of all Axis forces in northern Italy some three and a half years hence. Although there were some local suc-

Aircraft of I./StG 3 still follow the coast to the scene of the action

Arguably the best known – and most photographed – Stuka of the desert campaign was I./StG 1's Ju 87R 'A5+HL'. Here it is fully loaded for the next mission . . .

. . . and this is how Allied troops found it – derelict and abandoned, late in 1941

Tail and wings dismantled, propeller blades sawn through, 'HL' ends its days in an aircraft dump alongside erstwhile allies and enemies (note Macchi MC 200 and Hurricane in background left). 'Hans Huckebein' (the diving bird on the engine cowling) has obviously withstood somebody's attempt to remove him as a souvenir!

cesses still to be achieved in the months ahead, throughout this time the Junkers dive-bomber would be a steadily declining force on the field of battle, overtaken by events, overshadowed by the rise of the fighter-bomber and overwhelmed by the enemy's growing numerical superiority.

The first engagement of the New Year was a sign of things to come. Attacked by Australian Kittyhawks south-east of Agedabia on 1 January 1942, 16 Stukas immediately jettisoned their bombs and went into a defensive circle, which failed to prevent nearly half their number being destroyed or damaged. A fortnight later some semblance of order was introduced into the desert Stuka arm when I./StG 1 and II./StG 2 were officially incorporated into StG 3 (Oberleutnant Sigel's hitherto single-*Gruppe Geschwader*) by being redesignated II. and III./StG 3 respectively.

The 'new' StG 3 was just in time to support the launch of Rommel's

57

The officer seen here seated to the left during a visit by *General der Flieger* Geisler to II./StG 2 at Tmimi in December 1941 is Leutnant Hubert Pölz, who piloted one of the most spectacularly painted Stukas in the desert (see profile 11)

Although of poor quality, these two pictures suffice to show that there were at least two different such snake motifs applied

'Ride 'em cowboy!' A member of the groundcrew attempts to bring down to earth the tail of this 2./StG 3 machine, which presumably nosed over during take-off – note the full load of bombs (just visible under the wing) still aboard!

But more and more Stukas were ending their days in dumps like these, left behind to be found by advancing British and Commonwealth troops. Note the row of engineless Bf 109s in the background of the photograph below

surprise counter-offensive. The wily 'Desert Fox' had been withdrawing his troops ahead of the recent British advances (after a slow start, *Crusader* forces had covered the last 400 kms from Derna to Benghazi in just five days!), and on 21 January he suddenly struck back north of El Agheila. Eight days later he re-occupied Benghazi – the fourth time the Cyrenaican capital had changed hands in a year – and unleashed his Panzers towards Egypt again. This time they would drive deep into British territory, coming to within 100 kms of Alexandria, before finally being stopped at a tiny wayside halt on the coastal railway called El Alamein.

Taking advantage of the enemy's initial disarray, StG 3 ranged ahead of Rommel's spearheads, attacking the retreating columns and seeking to

59

Aside from the many captured on the ground, a number of Stukas were forced down behind enemy lines. This dejected looking pair are surrendering to a rather nonplussed Rhodesian Army sergeant

disrupt the British lines of communication. Within weeks they were back over Tobruk, and it was here, as their losses were beginning to rise again, that Knight's Cross holder Hauptmann Helmut Naumann, *Kommandeur* of I./StG 3, would be seriously wounded on 27 March.

But while I. and II. *Gruppen* were busy engaging desert targets and shipping in and around Tobruk, Major Enneccerus' III./StG 3 had been withdrawn across the Mediterranean to San Pancrazio, where they became the first to convert to the new and improved Ju 87D, or 'Dora'. They were then retained on Sicily, under II. *Fliegerkorps*, to participate in the renewed assault on Malta. The island had undergone sporadic night attacks from 101° *Gruppo*'s Picchiatelli throughout much of the latter half of 1941, but these raids had not prevented Malta's gradual reinforcement. Now a fresh attempt was to be made to neutralise this threat to Rommel's seaborne supply lines.

The brunt of the 1942 offensive was to be borne by Axis bomber forces. But despite the presence of Spitfires on the island, both German and Italian dive-bombers would also be called upon to play their part. III./StG 3's 24 March attack on Hal Far airfield heralded eight weeks of intensive operations. They suffered the inevitable losses, but chalked up several successes too, most notably against naval units sheltering in the Grand Harbour. On 1 April they sank the supply submarine *Pandora* with two direct hits, while several near misses caused the submarine *P 36* to founder. Four days later the destroyers *Lance* and *Gallant* were sunk in dock. A third destroyer, *Kingston,* was severely damaged on 11 April. By mid-May the *Gruppe* had been reduced to almost half-strength. The survivors ended their association with Malta as they had begun it, attacking Hal Far on 13

May. The following week they were back at Bir el Hania, in North Africa.

On 28 May – ten days after III./StG 3's departure – the Picchiatelli reappeared over Malta, four Ju 87s of 239ᵃ *Squadriglia* attacking the island's airfields under cover of darkness. The following night it was the turn of four 209ᵃ *Squadriglia* machines. These two units, which had formerly operated as 97° *Gruppo*, had been remustered on 1 May as the new 102° *Gruppo* under the command of the redoubtable Giuseppe Cenni. For the next six months (like 101° *Gruppo* before them) they would continue to harass Malta by night. And together with elements of StG 3, they would also play a role in two forthcoming convoy actions.

In the desert, meanwhile, Rommel's forces were making slow, but steady, progress. They had retaken the Derna airfields in mid-February, allowing the Stukas to move forward in support. By mid-May the leading Panzers had 'bumped' the Gazala Line. This line – more accurately a succession of fortified 'boxes', each surrounded by wire and deep minefields – stretched south-eastwards across some 55 kms of desert from El Gazala, on the coast, to the old desert fort of Bir Hacheim. It had been established in an attempt to halt the Axis advance. A Luftwaffe war correspondent wrote a somewhat colourful account of a Stuka raid on one such 'box';

'A narrow strip of no-man's land and then we were over enemy territory. There far below was the target. At least 200 British vehicles gathered in a large square, surrounded by numerous flak batteries.

'Although we're still many thousands of metres above them, the flak has already opened fire. The formation opens out and begins the "Flak Waltz", weaving between the hundreds of deadly cotton-wool balls being aimed up at us.

'The first machine dives into the seething abyss. The rest follow. Flames erupt, vehicles explode, the guns fall silent. Like a beacon of destruction, a black column of smoke rises out of the swirling clouds of sand below. In seconds it's all over. Then it's back to base to

Crowds gather to wave off the crew of Picchiatello '4' as they prepare for another strike against Malta

Also operational over Malta during 1942 were elements of StG 3. Here, pilots of I. *Gruppe* greet the ubiquitous *General der Flieger Geisler* on a Sicilian airfield – whose background looks suspiciously like Trapani

start all over again. Several times a day the same procedure – take-off, target, release bomb, land, reload, take-off . . . The defenders' fire grew progressively weaker. All our *Ketten* returned safely, the last landing as the blood-red ball of the sun sank into the sand sea.'

Such descriptive passages may have reassured the home readership, but the reality was far different. At least three Stukas were lost to anti-aircraft fire on that 26 May, including one III. *Gruppe* machine only recently returned from operations over Malta. But it was at the southern end of the Gazala Line that the desert Stukas enjoyed their last triumph. Garrisoned by a force of Free French troops under Gen Koenig, the fort of Bir Hacheim was subjected to 14 days of pounding by dive-bombers, artillery and Panzers. Despite being isolated, the French refused to surrender, survivors holding out until, on 10 June, they were ordered to withdraw and fight their way back to British lines.

This was the last set-piece battle in North Africa in which the Ju 87 played a decisive part. But success had come at a price. Among StG 3's many losses over Bir Hacheim was another Knight's Cross holder, Hauptmann Heinrich Eppen, *Kommandeur* of I. *Gruppe*, who had fallen victim to South African Tomahawks on 4 June.

Seventy-two hours after the taking of Bir Hacheim, action switched back out to sea. Operation *Vigorous* was a convoy which sailed from Alexandria with supplies for Malta. On 13 June II./StG 3 – now also equipped with Ju 87Ds – took off from Derna. In the company of Ju 88s they discovered and sank a straggler from the convoy making for Tobruk, but lost two of their own number, including the *Kapitän* of 6. *Staffel*, Oberleutnant Anton Ostler, to the merchantman's escorting destroyers.

The following day 17 Picchiatelli of 102° *Gruppo* from Sicily engaged the main body of the convoy without result, as too did III./StG 3 from Derna, the latter also losing two aircraft. It was a different story on 15 June when both II. and III. *Gruppen* attacked the convoy in continuous waves. They damaged a number of vessels, including the ancient *Centurion* (the Fleet's pre-war wireless-controlled target-ship, which had been sent along to masquerade as a battleship!), the cruisers *Arethusa* and *Birmingham*, and the destroyers *Airedale* and *Nestor* – the last pair so seriously that they had to be sunk. Faced with these and other losses, and with the threat of interception by capital units of the Italian Fleet which were at sea hunting for it, the convoy was recalled to Alexandria.

Had the *Vigorous* straggler indeed succeeded in making Tobruk, her crew would have been in for a nasty surprise. After breaking through the Gazala Line, Rommel's forces finally reached the town's outer perimeter defences on 19 June. An assault was launched on 20 June . . . and Tobruk fell on 21 June!

There were fierce recriminations in the Allied camp over how a posi-

A Luftwaffe war correspondent (right), cuff title just visible on his right sleeve, poses with the pilot before a flight in a Stuka of StG 3 (note the bomb on the ground behind fuselage step). The kapok life-jackets presumably indicate an overwater mission, about which the pilot looks none too pleased – or perhaps he's just squinting into the sun!

tion which had withstood an eight-month siege the previous year could be taken in just twenty-four hours, but by then Rommel was already charging into Egypt. On 1 July he began his attack on the Allies' next line of defence at El Alamein. But Alamein was no Gazala. Although only marginally longer than the Gazala defences, the line which stretched southwards from the coast at El Alamein did not end at an ancient fort in the open desert. Instead, it was firmly anchored on the Qattara Depression, a huge hollow in the desert some 250 kms in length – much of it below sea-level – whose soft surface would not support armoured vehicles. Impossible to be outflanked, Alamein was the perfect defensive position. And it was here – under a new commander, Lt-Gen Bernard Montgomery, who vowed there would not be another step back – that the British 8th Army made its stand.

For nearly four months the opposing forces faced each other, either side building up its strength for the decisive blow. It was therefore not only to revictual Malta, but also to enhance the island's capability to disrupt Rommel's supply lines across the Mediterranean, that a new convoy, Operation *Pedestal*, was assembled. Unlike *Vigorous*, however, the 14 merchantmen of *Pedestal* would approach Malta from the west, and they would be supported by more than just a dummy battleship – in fact, the immediate covering and escort forces comprised no fewer than two battleships, three Fleet carriers, seven cruisers and thirty-two destroyers!

Learning of the approach of this veritable armada, the Axis deployed their naval and air units accordingly. The fact that Ju 87s accounted for fewer than 40 of the more than 650 aircraft being amassed is perhaps a reflection of the dive-bomber's diminishing significance and reputation. But the 13 Picchiatelli of 102° *Gruppo* which had been transferred to the island of Pantelleria – right in the path of the oncoming convoy – and the 26 Doras of I./StG 3, sent from North Africa to Trapani and Sciacca in western Sicily, would give a good account of themselves.

On 12 August the dive-bombers attacked the main naval covering force. Twelve aircraft of I./StG 3 scored two direct hits and three near misses on the carrier *Indomitable*, putting her flightdeck out of action.

Oberstleutnant Walter Sigel's *Geschwaderstab* 'Dora' 'S7+AA' against the unmistakable backdrop of the Siwa Oasis settlement. Situated at the south-western extremity of the Qattara Depression, Siwa was occupied by Axis forces for some four months between July and November 1942

Two Stukas failed to return. 102° *Gruppo* also lost two aircraft that day, one of which was hit by anti-aircraft fire and crashed on the stern of the battleship *Rodney*. Next morning, while attacking the merchantmen, another Picchiatelli fell victim to anti-aircraft gunners. It hit the sea close alongside the already grievously damaged tanker *Ohio*, bounced off the rolling swell and smashed down on to her foredeck. Despite this, and further attacks by the Picchiatelli while under tow the following day, the *Ohio* limped into Malta to unload her precious cargo of aviation fuel. The motor vessel *Dorset* was less fortunate. She was set ablaze by Stukas of I./StG 3 on that same 13 August and had to be abandoned – 24 hours later the *Gruppe* damaged the cruiser *Kenya*. Shortly after the passage of the convoy, the Ju 87s returned whence they came – 102° *Gruppo* to Sicily to resume their nocturnal raids on Malta and I./StG 3 back to the desert.

Of the convoy's 14 merchant vessels, five arrived in Malta. The 32,000 tons of cargo they delivered paid immediate dividends, for Axis shipping losses to Malta-based air attack began to rise and Rommel's supply shortages grew acute.

From their landing grounds around Fuka and Quasaba, deep inside Egypt (and less than 150 kms from the Alamein positions), the Stukas of StG 3 were now mounting operations almost daily. But the mystique had evaporated. A British report dismissed the Ju 87 as 'nothing more than a psychological instrument of terror, capable of only local and isolated destruction, ineffective against resolute troops and highly vulnerable to our fighters'. Even the *Staffelkapitän* of 5./StG 3, Oberleutnant Hans Drescher, admitted that 'the position of the English at El Alamein could no longer be penetrated'.

Nevertheless the 'Doras' continued to attack British troop concentrations, gun emplacements and tank laagers with stubborn ferocity. But with their radio traffic being monitored (the RAF, well aware by now that the Stukas' call signs were *'Wespe'* – 'Wasp' – and *'Isar'* – Munich's river – were listening out for any exchange of messages between the dive-bombers and their escorts) and increasing numbers of Allied fighters on the prowl, it is hardly surprising that their losses began to escalate sharply.

More and more frequently the Stukas were being forced to jettison their bombs and turn back to base (although the story that a diary found on a captured *Afrika Korps* officer contained the entry, '*Gott in Himmel*, bombed *again* by the Luftwaffe' is probably apocryphal!). And even when they did return to their bases, they were not much safer. Marauding enemy fighters and fighter-bombers exacted a steady toll of Stukas destroyed or damaged on the ground, or while taking off and landing. Nor were these the only dangers. Jeep patrols of the Long Range Desert Group, operating far behind Axis lines, were not averse to shooting up somnolent Luftwaffe landing grounds at night. One such attack on Quasaba cost StG 3 five 'Doras' completely destroyed, plus another seven badly damaged.

At 21.40 hours on the night of 23 October 1942 the Western Desert was lit up by the fire from over 1000 British guns. It was the greatest artillery barrage since World War 1 – Montgomery had won the supply battle. The third 'Benghazi Stakes' were about to be run, and this time there would be no coming back.

It nonetheless took the 8th Army a good ten days to break through the

Axis crust. During this period of concentrated and almost constant daylight air action Allied fighter pilots claimed the destruction of some 40 Ju 87s, plus as many again 'probables' and damaged. One of the early victims was another experienced *Gruppenkommandeur* and Knight's Cross holder. Hauptmann Kurt Walter, who had taken over Walter Enneccerus' place at the head of III./StG 3, and who had been instrumental in sinking the anti-aircraft cruiser *Coventry* and destroyer *Zulu* off Tobruk on 14 September, was caught by fighters at dusk on 26 October while landing after the last of that day's raids. Walter baled out, but had insufficient altitude for his parachute to open properly.

By 11 November the 8th Army had reached the Halfaya Pass – the route up the escarpment out of Egypt on to the plateau of the Libyan Desert. Here the Luftwaffe made one last desperate attempt to halt the advancing Allied armour. At dawn 15 Stukas of I./StG 3 led the assault. They were pounced upon by a squadron of South African Kittyhawks, who claimed 12 of them, the surviving trio being shot down by patrolling American P-40Fs as they tried to land back at Gambut. Among the former casualties was yet one more Knight's Cross *Kommandeur*. Hauptmann Martin Mossdorf had assumed command of I. *Gruppe* after 'Hein' Eppen's loss over Bir Hacheim. Mossdorf, however, managed to crash-land his burning 'Dora', and both he and his wireless-operator were taken prisoner.

This virtual annihilation of I./StG 3 spelled the end for the Stuka in the Western Desert. The survivors were withdrawn to Germany for re-equipment, after which the *Gruppe* would be deployed to the Eastern Front.

This 'Dora' of 8./StG 3 force-landed behind Allied lines after being attacked by fighters on 1 November, its wounded crew being taken prisoner. Note the aft section of the cockpit glazing on the ground in the shadow of the tail, and the signs of current action in the left background

One of III. *Gruppe*'s aircraft which covered Rommel's retreat across Libya during the closing weeks of 1942 . . .

. . . many didn't make it, however, as witness this example, which fell intact into Allied hands. The spinner-less 'Dora' in US insignia was photographed at Castel Benito, some 24 km south of Tripoli, in February 1943

II./StG 3 was likewise transferred to Sardinia for rest and refit. Only the rump of III. *Gruppe* remained to cover the Afrika Korps' final retreat across Libya. But even before this had begun, a new danger had erupted far in the German rear. Operation *Torch* – the landing of Anglo-American forces in Morocco and Algeria on 8 November 1942 – was designed to be the other half of a giant pincer movement from both east and west, which would squeeze the Axis out of Africa altogether.

Luftwaffe units were rushed in to Vichy-held Tunisia to counter this latest threat. Among them were the 24 'Doras' of II./StG 3, who staged via Sicily to Tunis-El Aouina, the large civil and military airfield just outside the country's capital. But they did not stay here for long, moving up to Djedeida before the month was out. (102° *Gruppo*, with exactly two serviceable Picchiatelli on Sicily, were in no state to participate in further operations at this stage).

II./StG 3 began taking casualties right from the outset. Tunisia was a fighter-bomber's war. Once a Bf 109 or Fw 190 had released its bomb load, it could at least choose either to retire or, if forced to, stay and defend itself against enemy fighters on something approaching equal terms. The Stukas enjoyed no such option. 6./StG 3 lost two *Staffelkapitäne* in little over a fortnight. But the greatest damage inflicted on the *Gruppe* in a single day occurred on 26 November when 17 tanks of the US 1st Armoured Division broke through to Djedeida and caused havoc, shooting up a number of 'Doras' at dispersal, ramming and crushing the tail units of others, and destroying yet more in the field's hangars and repair shops. Altogether, the Americans claimed the destruction of 36 Stukas (the Germans later admitting the loss of 15).

The material losses were quickly made good and II./StG 3 was soon back in the air. But it was finding itself ever more on the defensive, retir-

ing to Tunis and frequently unable to attack its assigned objectives. Instead it was being forced – as at Alamein – to jettison its bombs prematurely as the only hope of survival in northern Tunisia's increasingly hostile airspace. The *Gruppe*'s one significant success was the damage inflicted upon the cruiser *Ajax* during a combined Stuka and fighter-bomber raid on Bône harbour in Algeria on New Year's Day 1943.

Meanwhile III. *Gruppe* had completed their long trek back across Libya and had crossed into Tunisia in the far south. Based at Gabes, they were safe for the moment behind the frontier defences of the Mareth Line. Originally constructed by the French against attack from their Italian colonial neighbours (and since strengthened by the Germans), the Mareth Line was a mirror image of the Alamein position, running from Gabes on the coast to a salt marsh inland. From here, III./StG 3 spent several weeks flying missions over the southern Tunisian front, striking at targets as far afield as Gafsa, Sbeitla and Kasserine.

Although secure against surprise tank attack (such as that suffered by II./StG 3 in Djedeida), the Mareth Line offered III. *Gruppe* no protection against Allied bombing raids, and these grew in intensity as Montgomery prepared to storm the position and enter Tunisia from the south. III./StG 3 remained at Gabes until 26 February 1943. But when the field came under long-range artillery fire as well as aerial bombardment, it was time to move. Their base for the next month was Mezouna. By now their losses were

One of StG 3's indispensable DFS 230 supply gliders bearing the original I. *Gruppe* badge and Wk-Nr 227525

mounting too, and missions were being flown only when there was sufficient cloud cover to offer a chance of escape from the hordes of Allied fighters.

On 28 March the 8th Army finally breached the Mareth Line and struck northwards. For III./StG 3 this meant another withdrawal to El Djem. The *Gruppe* TO described the conditions of the time;

'We were being pushed back closer and closer to Tunis and the cape. The enemy's armoured spearheads were already approaching Kairouan. Operations were now only flown in *Rotte* or *Kette* strength – in other words, each mission consisted of just two or three aircraft. We had to keep our formations small and manoeuvrable if we wanted to reach the target.

'My *Kette*'s orders were to attack the Panzers near Kairouan. Eight-tenths cloud, so a stealthy approach – sometimes above the cloud layer, sometimes below. Everywhere you looked the opposition's fighters. There – one has seen us. Nothing for it but to dive into the white soup below. My wingmen follow me down. The cloud base was only some 200 metres above ground. Diving at a shallow angle, I try to peer through it – nothing. We finally break through about 80 metres from the ground, but find ourselves surrounded on all sides by mountains! Nothing for it but to climb back up, and fast. We emerge into clear air again. A quick look around. Not an aircraft in sight.'

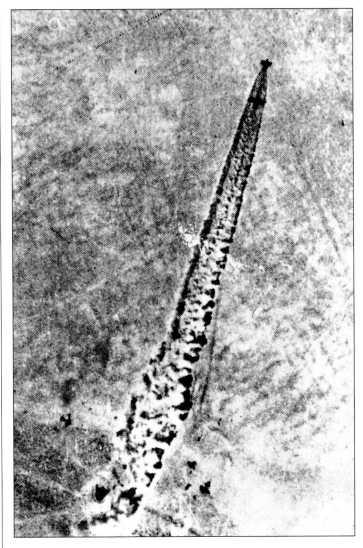

This Ju 87/DFS 230 combination was caught on camera by an RAF PR aircraft whilst in the process of taking off from a desert airstrip

The *Kette* never did locate the tanks, but stumbled instead across a target of opportunity – a column of soft-skinned vehicles 'stretching as far as the eye could see'. After bombing and strafing, all three returned safely to El Djem, only to be caught in the latest heavy bomber raid on the field before they even had time to taxy to dispersal.

After less than a fortnight III./StG 3 were forced to evacuate El Djem. Their third and final move, on 8 April, took them to Oudna, only some 20 kms from Tunis, and the remnants of II. *Gruppe*. The last missions were flown the following day – three sorties against US armour north of Kairouan. By this stage the situation had deteriorated to such an extent that Luftwaffe fighters had only enough fuel to protect the Stukas during the few vulnerable minutes of take-off. Once they were aloft the 'Doras' were on their own.

On 10 and 11 April the Stukas did not manage to get into the air at all. They remained pinned to the ground in the heavily camouflaged revetments which were their only protection against marauding Allied fighters. Twenty-four hours later the surviving 'Doras' began to evacuate Africa. Singly and in small groups, they set out across the narrows separating the tip of Tunisia from the already somewhat uncertain safety of Sicily. The wheel had turned full circle. Over the very waters where their predecessors had pitted their massed strength against the Malta convoys, individual 'Doras' now sought to slip through undetected by the standing Allied air patrols.

Perhaps the last Stuka loss of the African campaign was the hapless 'Dora' of II./StG 3 discovered on 19 April towing one of the transport gliders which had been of such service to the desert *Stukagruppen* during their many moves from one landing ground to the next. This combination stood no chance against the three squadrons of South African Kittyhawks which found it. Both tug and glider went down into the sea off Cape Bon.

So ended 15 months of hard desert fighting by the Ju 87s, with little to show for their passage except a trail of crashed, wrecked and abandoned Stuka carcasses littering the coastal belt of North Africa from the sands of El Alamein to the mountains of Tunisia.

COLOUR PLATES

This 12-page colour section profiles many of the aircraft flown in combat by the *Stukageschwader* (and *Regia Aeronautica*) in the Mediterranean, North Africa and southern Europe between 1941 and 1945. All the artwork has been specially commissioned for this volume, and profile artist John Weal and figure artist Mike Chappell have gone to great pains to illustrate the aircraft, and their crews, as accurately as possible following in-depth research from original sources. Ju 87s that have never previously been seen in profile are featured alongside acccurate renditions of some of the more familiar Stukas of the period. The profiles appear in unit establishment order.

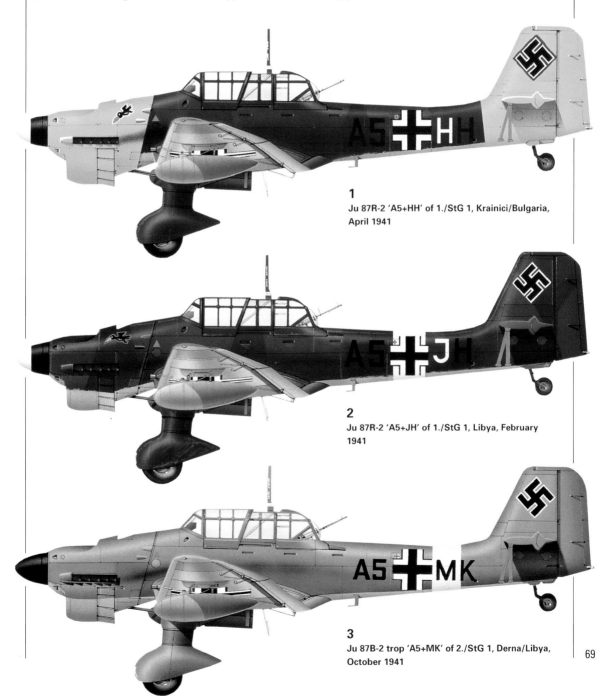

1
Ju 87R-2 'A5+HH' of 1./StG 1, Krainici/Bulgaria, April 1941

2
Ju 87R-2 'A5+JH' of 1./StG 1, Libya, February 1941

3
Ju 87B-2 trop 'A5+MK' of 2./StG 1, Derna/Libya, October 1941

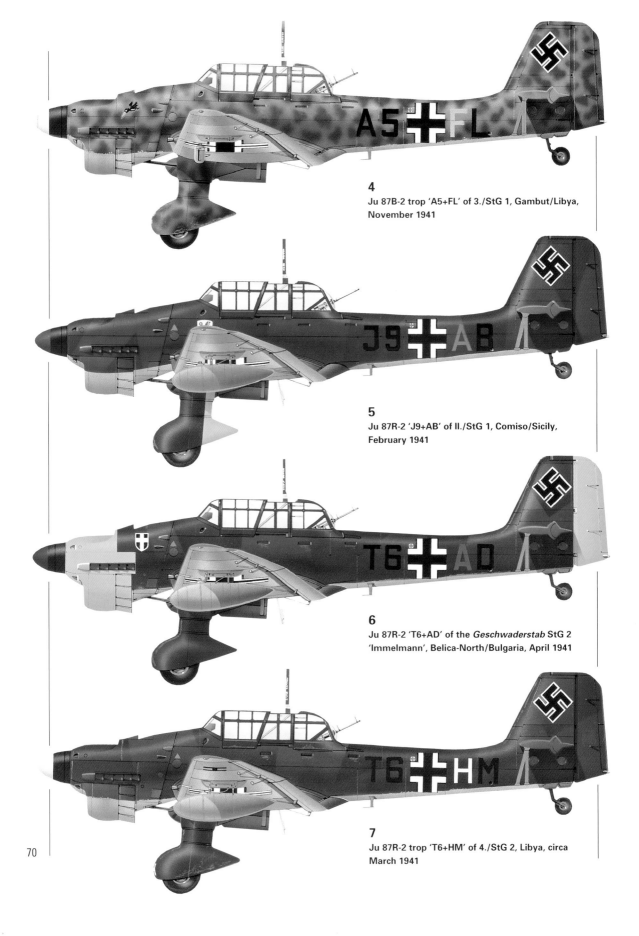

4
Ju 87B-2 trop 'A5+FL' of 3./StG 1, Gambut/Libya,
November 1941

5
Ju 87R-2 'J9+AB' of II./StG 1, Comiso/Sicily,
February 1941

6
Ju 87R-2 'T6+AD' of the *Geschwaderstab* StG 2
'Immelmann', Belica-North/Bulgaria, April 1941

7
Ju 87R-2 trop 'T6+HM' of 4./StG 2, Libya, circa
March 1941

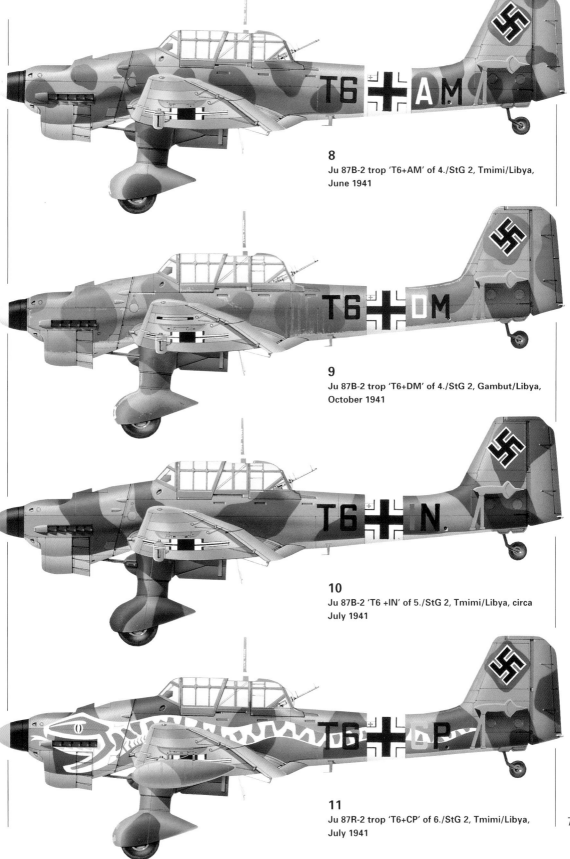

8
Ju 87B-2 trop 'T6+AM' of 4./StG 2, Tmimi/Libya,
June 1941

9
Ju 87B-2 trop 'T6+DM' of 4./StG 2, Gambut/Libya,
October 1941

10
Ju 87B-2 'T6 +IN' of 5./StG 2, Tmimi/Libya, circa
July 1941

11
Ju 87R-2 trop 'T6+CP' of 6./StG 2, Tmimi/Libya,
July 1941

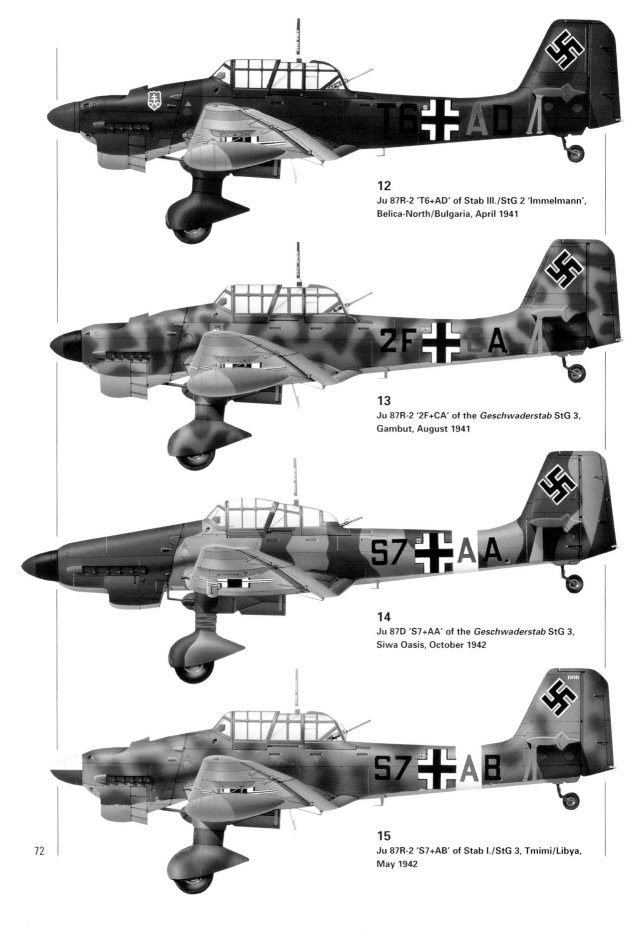

12
Ju 87R-2 'T6+AD' of Stab III./StG 2 'Immelmann',
Belica-North/Bulgaria, April 1941

13
Ju 87R-2 '2F+CA' of the *Geschwaderstab* StG 3,
Gambut, August 1941

14
Ju 87D 'S7+AA' of the *Geschwaderstab* StG 3,
Siwa Oasis, October 1942

15
Ju 87R-2 'S7+AB' of Stab I./StG 3, Tmimi/Libya,
May 1942

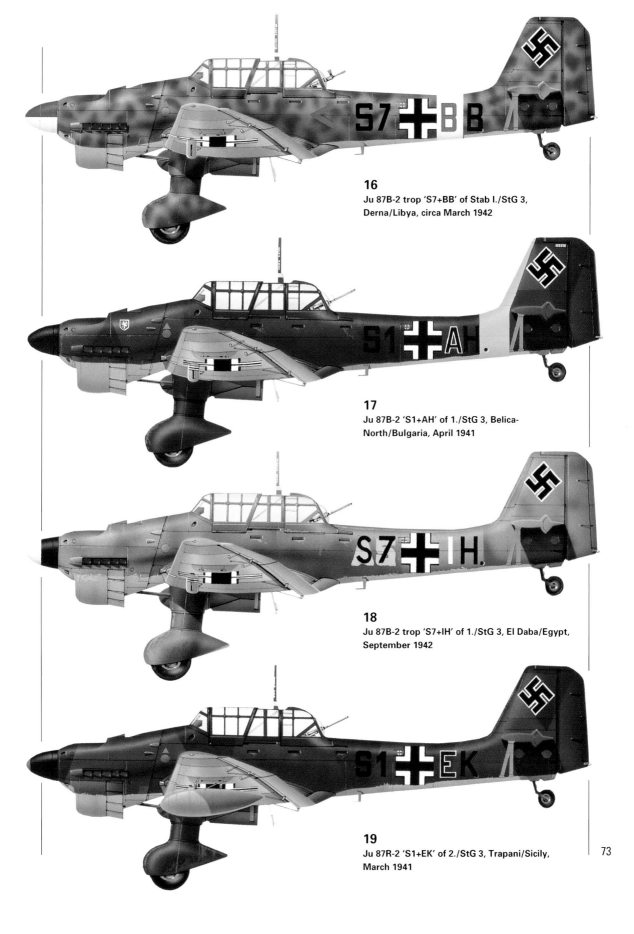

16
Ju 87B-2 trop 'S7+BB' of Stab I./StG 3,
Derna/Libya, circa March 1942

17
Ju 87B-2 'S1+AH' of 1./StG 3, Belica-
North/Bulgaria, April 1941

18
Ju 87B-2 trop 'S7+IH' of 1./StG 3, El Daba/Egypt,
September 1942

19
Ju 87R-2 'S1+EK' of 2./StG 3, Trapani/Sicily,
March 1941

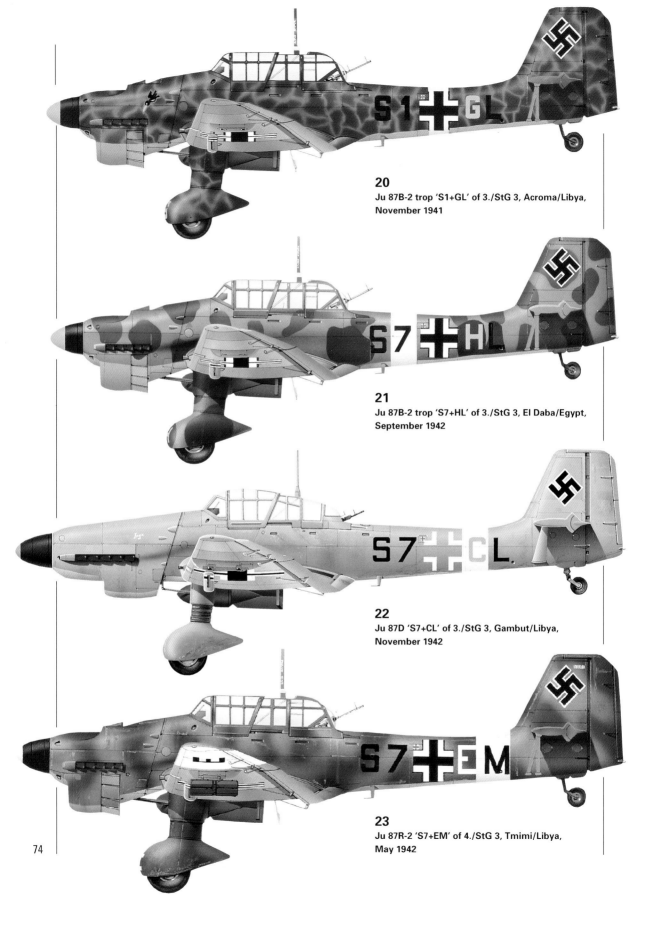

20
Ju 87B-2 trop 'S1+GL' of 3./StG 3, Acroma/Libya,
November 1941

21
Ju 87B-2 trop 'S7+HL' of 3./StG 3, El Daba/Egypt,
September 1942

22
Ju 87D 'S7+CL' of 3./StG 3, Gambut/Libya,
November 1942

23
Ju 87R-2 'S7+EM' of 4./StG 3, Tmimi/Libya,
May 1942

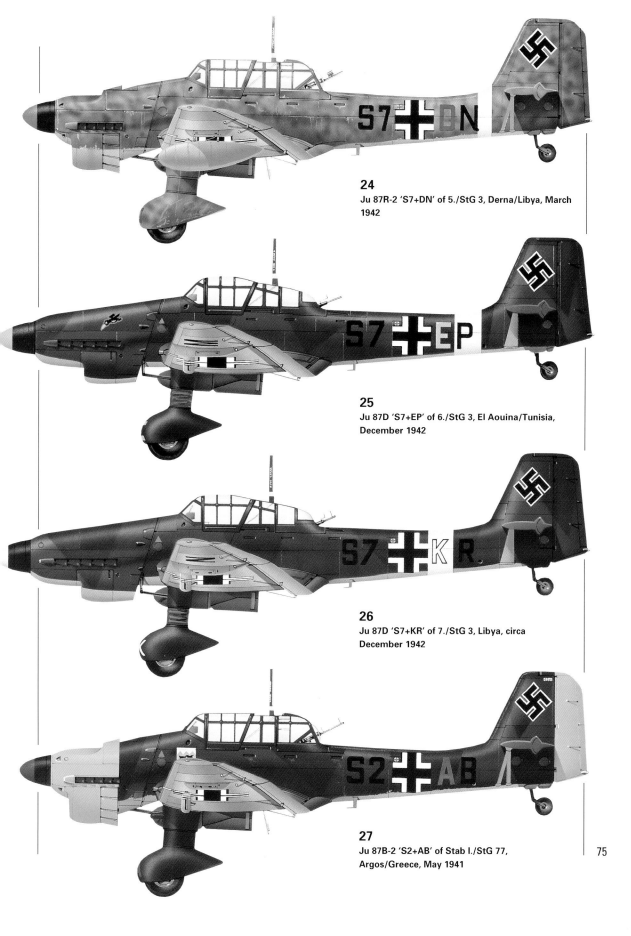

24
Ju 87R-2 'S7+DN' of 5./StG 3, Derna/Libya, March 1942

25
Ju 87D 'S7+EP' of 6./StG 3, El Aouina/Tunisia, December 1942

26
Ju 87D 'S7+KR' of 7./StG 3, Libya, circa December 1942

27
Ju 87B-2 'S2+AB' of Stab I./StG 77, Argos/Greece, May 1941

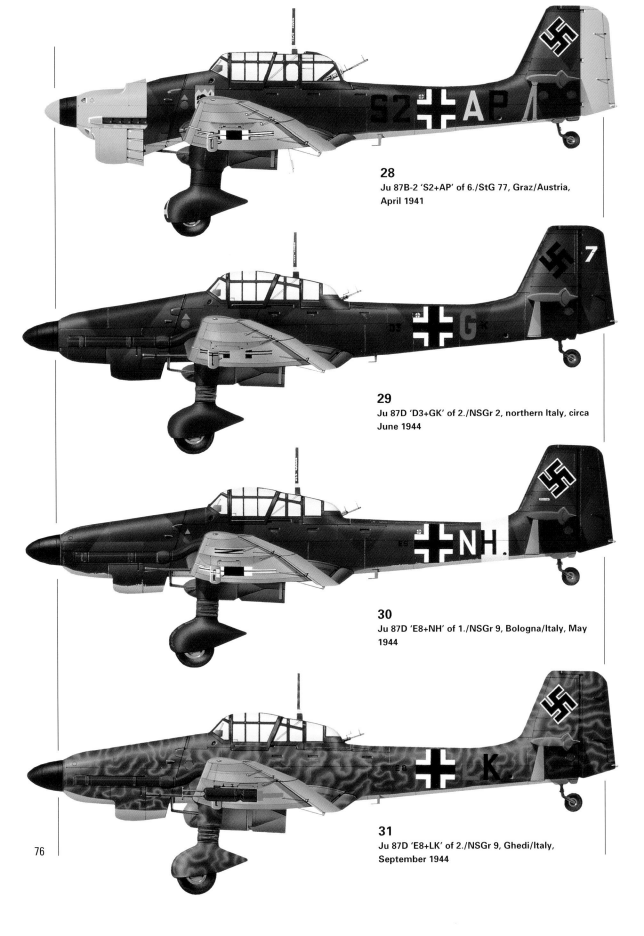

28
Ju 87B-2 'S2+AP' of 6./StG 77, Graz/Austria,
April 1941

29
Ju 87D 'D3+GK' of 2./NSGr 2, northern Italy, circa
June 1944

30
Ju 87D 'E8+NH' of 1./NSGr 9, Bologna/Italy, May
1944

31
Ju 87D 'E8+LK' of 2./NSGr 9, Ghedi/Italy,
September 1944

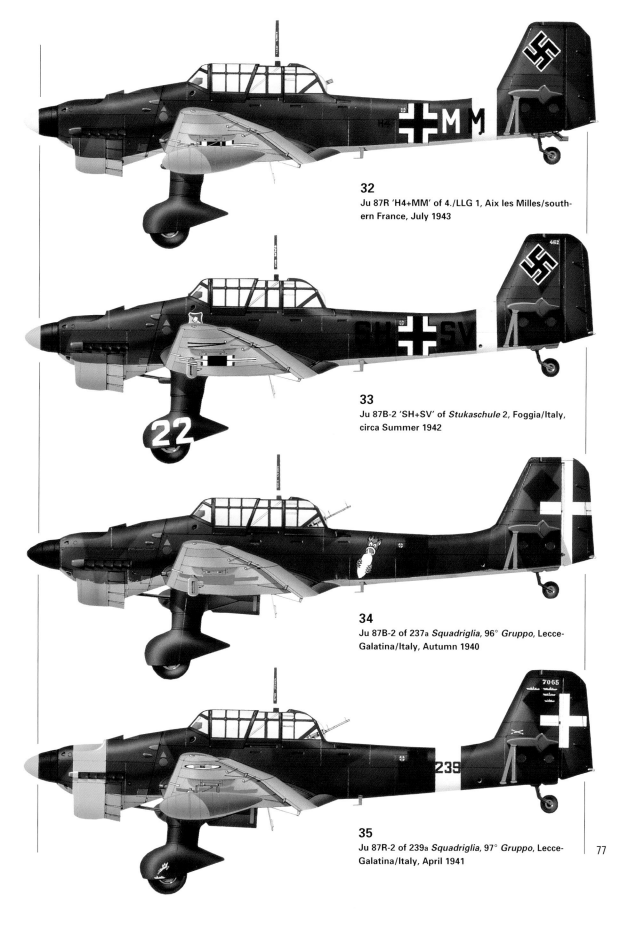

32
Ju 87R 'H4+MM' of 4./LLG 1, Aix les Milles/southern France, July 1943

33
Ju 87B-2 'SH+SV' of *Stukaschule* 2, Foggia/Italy, circa Summer 1942

34
Ju 87B-2 of 237a *Squadriglia*, 96° *Gruppo*, Lecce-Galatina/Italy, Autumn 1940

35
Ju 87R-2 of 239a *Squadriglia*, 97° *Gruppo*, Lecce-Galatina/Italy, April 1941

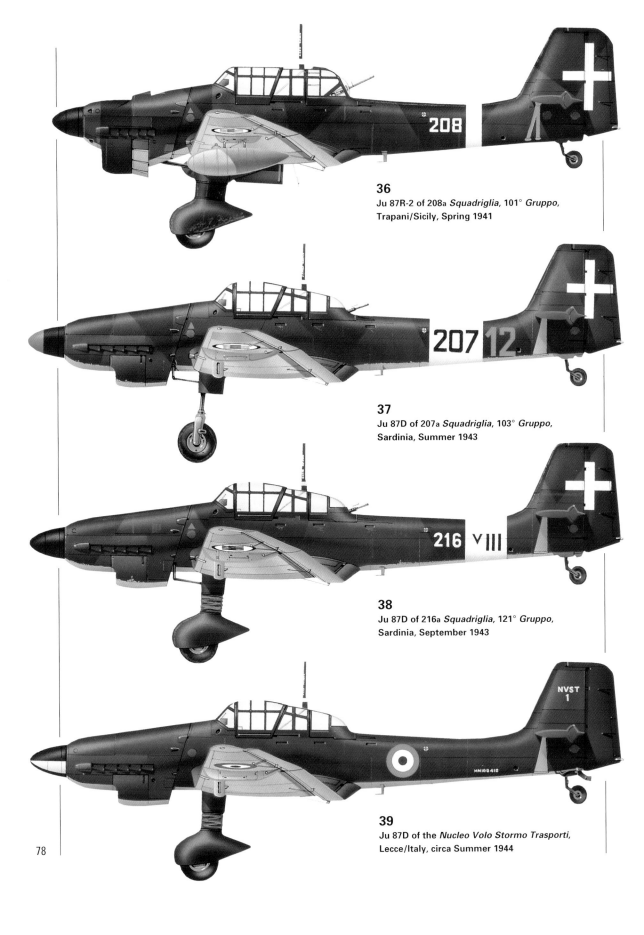

36
Ju 87R-2 of 208a *Squadriglia*, 101° *Gruppo*,
Trapani/Sicily, Spring 1941

37
Ju 87D of 207a *Squadriglia*, 103° *Gruppo*,
Sardinia, Summer 1943

38
Ju 87D of 216a *Squadriglia*, 121° *Gruppo*,
Sardinia, September 1943

39
Ju 87D of the *Nucleo Volo Stormo Trasporti*,
Lecce/Italy, circa Summer 1944

1
Oberleutnant Hartmut Schairer,
Staffelkapitän of 7/StG 1,
Comiso/Sicily, February 1941

2
Maggiore Giuseppe Donadio,
Comandante of 101° *Gruppo* B.aT.,
Tirana/Albania, April 1941

3
Hauptmann Helmut Mahlke,
Gruppenkommandeur of III./StG 1,
Derna/Libya, April 1941

4
Major Walter Enneccerus,
Gruppenkommandeur of II./StG 2,
Tmimi/Libya, Summer 1941

5
Oberstleutnant Walter Sigel,
Geschwaderkommodore of StG 3,
Siwa Oasis/Egypt, September 1942

6
Oberleutnant Herbert Stry,
Staffelkapitän of 5./StG 3,
Martuba/Libya, April 1942

OPERATIONS IN SOUTHERN EUROPE

The end of the North African campaign inevitably meant a sharp decline in the number of operational dive-bomber units in the Mediterranean. But the Ju 87 did not disappear from the theatre altogether. In fact, the coming autumn would witness a brief resurgence in the Stukas' fortunes when, for nearly eight weeks, two of StG 3's *Gruppen* would experience a level of local superiority reminiscent of the glory days of the *Blitzkrieg*.

In the immediate wake of the Tunisian evacuation Stab StG 3 (now commanded by Major Kurt Kuhlmey) and III./StG 3 had retired to Germany to rest and refit before transferring to the Eastern Front. II./StG 3 also withdrew, but only as far as the eastern Mediterranean. Therefore, when Allied forces crossed the narrows to launch Operation *Husky* (the invasion of Sicily) on 10 July 1943, the dive-bomber response was entirely in the hands of the Italians.

By this time, however, 102° *Gruppo* had completed conversion on to Reggiane Re 2002 fighter-bombers (101° *Gruppo* had long been operating the Fiat CR 42 in a similar role). The *Regia Aeronautica* had taken delivery of a batch of Ju 87Ds earlier in the year, but rather than re-equip their existing dive-bomber units, the 'Doras' had been used to form two new *gruppi* – 103° and 121°.

Although not the sharpest of photographs, this view is nonetheless significant for it is one of the very few in existence to show a 'Dora' of StG 3 in the eastern Mediterranean. After their recent experiences hiding from Allied fighters in Tunisia, II.*Gruppe* must have found such pristine expanses of wide open concrete hard to get used to

A *Kette* of bomb-laden 'Doras' is seen reportedly flying an anti-partisan mission over the mountains of Montenegro

Still working up on Sardinia, the largely inexperienced crews were despatched at once to southern Italy and Sicily to counter the invasion. Faced with massive Allied aerial supremacy, they suffered devastating losses. The only reported success is believed to have been the 1700-ton US destroyer *Maddox*, which was screening American vessels off the Gela invasion beach during the opening hours of the assault. A bomb from an unseen aircraft struck the destroyer's stern, blowing it apart 'in a gust of flame, smoke and debris'. In less than two minutes she had disappeared beneath the waves.

The surviving 'Doras' of 121° *Gruppo* were to retire back to Sardinia long before the Sicilian campaign had run its 38-day course. 103° *Gruppo* had simply ceased to exist. The next obvious step for the Allies was to cross the Straits of Messina, the three-kilometre stretch of water separating Sicily from the toe of Italy. This they did on 3 September. Six days later, as Anglo-American forces landed at Salerno and Taranto, the Italian government, having overthrown the Duce, announced an armistice.

For the last time Hitler came to the aid of his southern partner-in-arms. Mussolini was freed from captivity by a daring airborne raid on his hotel-prison on the Gran Sasso, the highest peak in the Apennines. Henceforth Italy would be split in two – the southern part on the side of the Allies, and the north (under Mussolini) continuing to support the Axis. The air arms of both factions would each deploy a handful of Ju 87Ds, but on second-line duties only.

The defection of the southern Italians brought the war to II./StG 3's doorstep. Stationed in Greece and on Crete, they were ideally situated to suppress those Italian garrisons on the offshore islands who were showing sympathy towards the Allied cause. Open revolt had already broken out on both Corfu and Cephalonia, on the west coast of Greece. It was while attacking Italian positions on the latter island that Knight's Cross holder Oberleutnant Herbert Stry, *Staffelkapitän* 6./StG 3, was killed on 21 September when the bomb he had just released exploded in mid-air.

But it would be to the east of Greece, among the Dodecanese Islands at the entrance to the Aegean where the Stuka dive-bomber really came back into its own. The resident German garrison on Rhodes, the main island of the group, had quickly overpowered the far more numerous Italians. British Prime Minister Winston Churchill, however (whose interest in the area, dating back to World War 1 and Gallipoli, bordered on the obsessive), was also anxious to exploit the current situation of unrest in the Aegean. At his urging, British troops were sent in to occupy a number of the other, smaller Dodecanese islands. The most important of these were Cos, Leros and Samos, all three of which were deeper into the Aegean *beyond* Rhodes. With the nearest RAF airfield some 500 kms away on Cyprus, it was a recipe for disaster.

The Germans reacted with their usual swiftness. A strong Luftwaffe contingent was assembled, including Stab and I./StG 3, who were brought back from Russia to join II. *Gruppe*. Based in Greece, Crete and on Rhodes itself, a strike force of some 75 Stukas soon ringed the Dodecanese, ready to support the planned German recapture of those islands seized by the British, and to attack shipping attempting to supply them.

The first target was Cos. Here was situated the sole airstrip available to the RAF. And a small number of Spitfires had, in fact, been flown in. But they had been overwhelmed in the pre-invasion bombardment, and when the German landing force approached Cos on 3 October, the only opposition came from Cyprus-based Beaufighters. They claimed two of StG 3's 'Doras', but lost five of their own number in the process. Meanwhile, other 'Doras' were bombing and strafing any sign of movement on the roads surrounding the invasion beaches. The German troops were thus able to land almost unopposed, and the 'Doras' continued to give them close sup-

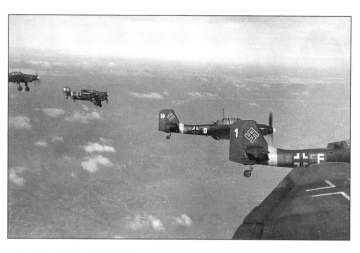

port as they quickly fanned out across the island. The Allied forces on Cos, comprising some 600 British and 2500 Italian personnel, surrendered 24 hours later.

Despite the loss of Cos (and its airstrip, which had offered the only hope of local air cover) the British continued to hold and supply their remaining islands. The next five weeks witnessed a succession of small-scale, but nonetheless fiercely fought, sea and air actions along the island chain. Many of these involved light coastal craft. But in a re-run of the Cretan campaign of more than two years earlier, the British were also sending in small 'task forces' of cruisers and destroyers under cover of darkness. Eighteen 'Doras' of I./StG 3 discovered one such group retiring through the Scarpanto Straits south of Rhodes on 7 October. They badly damaged the cruiser *Penelope* – a veteran of the Mediterranean Fleet who had been holed so many times she was nicknamed 'HMS Pepperpot', the *Penelope* regained Alexandria under her own power, but was out of action for three weeks.

Even before this force had returned to Alexandria, another was on its way to the Aegean. Forty-eight hours after the assault on the *Penelope*, all twenty-six serviceable 'Doras' of I./StG 3 lifted off to attack this new target, which by this time was also withdrawing through the straits between Scarpanto and Rhodes. The 1540-ton destroyer *Panther* suffered two direct hits and several near misses almost at once. Her back broken, she sank in two separate halves.

Meanwhile, the bulk of the Stukas were concentrating on the largest vessel in the group. This was the elderly anti-aircraft cruiser *Carlisle* (sister ship of the *Coventry*, sunk by III./StG 3 off Tobruk). She was hit by four bombs, and near-missed by two others. Severely damaged underwater, the *Carlisle* had to be towed back to Alexandria, where she served out the rest of the war as a base ship.

On this occasion, however, the

Unlike the three previous aircraft, these Ju 87s – high above similar terrain – carry large white numerals on their rudders, which mark them out as trainers. As both photographs were taken during the same period, they may possibly depict the *Einsatzstaffel* and a training formation of SG 151 respectively

Providing something of a puzzle, this late-production 'Dora' was purportedly photographed in Italy in 1943. It appears to be a 7.*Staffel* machine in Eastern Front markings, and what it was doing in the Mediterranean remains a mystery

83

No uncertainty about this Ju 87R, however. The DFS 230 glider in the foreground and the tow-hook attachment behind the tailwheel clearly identify it as a glider-tug of II./LLG 1

Doras did not escape unscathed. In the middle of their attack they were suddenly set upon by a formation of US P-38 Lightnings (which had flown across the Mediterranean from Gambut in Libya). Those Stukas which had nor yet released their bombs did so in a hurry and joined the rest in making a run for nearby Rhodes. Before they could reach it, the American fighters had claimed the destruction of 16 of them – seven by the Lightnings' squadron leader alone (see *Osprey Aircraft of the Aces 19 - P-38 Lightning Aces of the ETO/MTO* for more details). In reality, the number of dive-bombers which failed to return to base was eight.

Fortunately for the Stukas, the P-38s' intervention in the Dodecanese was short-lived. Unmolested except for the occasional Beaufighter, they concentrated on the next job in hand – softening up the defences of Leros, the second of the islands scheduled for invasion. It was at this juncture that the Luftwaffe's *Stukageschwader* underwent wholesale redesignation, combining with all the other ground-attack units to form the newly reorganised *Schlacht* arm. It was therefore as I. *Gruppe* of *Schlachtgeschwader* 3 (I./SG 3) that the 'Doras' found and damaged their third cruiser of the campaign – the *Aurora* – on 30 October.

Leros was invaded on 12 November. The defenders held out for five days, but the dive-bombers had been thorough. Practically every gun emplacement on the island had been knocked out or damaged, and now the 'Doras' reverted to the Stuka's classic role of providing close support for the troops on the ground. Aircraft from both *Gruppen* circled the battlefield continuously, awaiting their infantry's call, before screaming down to eliminate any pockets of resistance – less than 250 exhausted British troops managed to escape. Three days later, the British also evacuated Samos, whose Italian garrison subsequently surrendered after Stukas of II./SG 3 had attacked their positions at Tigani. Almost the entire Dodecanese chain would remain in German hands until war's end.

The British commanders had done the best they could with the forces available to them, but geography – and the Luftwaffe – had beaten them again. Their feelings can only be imagined when the arch-instigator of the whole sorry fiasco, Winston Churchill, distanced himself by complaining, 'Have we not failed to learn the lessons of Crete? Have we not restored the Stukas to a fleeting moment of their old triumphs?'

Their job done, the 'triumphant' Stab and I./SG 3 returned to the Eastern Front, this time taking II. *Gruppe* with them. Their departure meant the final disappearance of the daylight dive-bombing Stuka from the Mediterranean. But the bent-winged Junkers still equipped a number of Luftwaffe units based in countries bordering the northern shores of Mussolini's one-time *'mare nostrum'*.

There had long been several Stuka schools and training establishments in Italy itself, principally at Piacenza, San Damiano and Foggia. But on

17 May 1943 an entirely new unit was formed by the amalgamation of the *Ergänzungsgruppen* (OTU wings) of each of the five existing *Stukageschwader* into one centralised, five *Gruppe*-strong, training *Geschwader*. Designated StG 151, and commanded by Oberst Karl Christ, one-time *Kommodore* of StG 3, this unit was based at Agram (Zagreb), in Croatia, which, since the German invasion of April 1941, had split completely from the former Yugoslavia and was now an Axis satellite.

StG 151 had an establishment of 175 Ju 87s, and from the ranks of its instructors was formed an operational squadron for emergency use in times of crisis. This *Einsatzstaffel* StG 151 (which, after the October 1943 redesignations, would become 13./SG 151) saw widespread service on anti-partisan operations in the northern Balkans, and also participated briefly in the Dodecanese campaign.

In mid-June 1943 (a month after the activation of StG 151 in Croatia) a Ju 87 presence was established at the western end of the Mediterranean as well. The Luftwaffe's premier airborne landing unit, *Luftlandegeschwader* 1 (LLG 1), had returned to Germany earlier in the year after flying glider-supply missions on the Eastern Front. While at Halberstadt, II./LLG 1 had converted from their Hs 126 and Avia B-534 tug aircraft to Ju 87s. And it was with 24 Ju 87/DFS 230 glider-tug combinations that the *Gruppe*, under the command of Hauptmann Trautwein, then transferred to Aix les Milles, near Marseille, on the French Mediterranean coast.

In the aftermath of the German defeat in Tunisia, Trautwein's four *Staffeln*, together with the rest of the *Geschwader* (plus I./LLG 2), formed a mobile reserve ready to rush reinforcements to wherever the Allies might strike next – the odds being on Sardinia or Sicily. The Anglo-American invasion of the more distant island a month later precluded the short-legged Ju 87s from taking part in any of the major supply runs, but the *Gruppe* did fly several support missions to northern Italy. In September LLG 1 was withdrawn northwards. After wintering in Strasbourg-Polygon and Mannheim, II./LLG 1, now led by Major Jahnke, was ordered to Croatia in March 1944.

Based at Zierkli and Kraljevo, near Agram, the *Gruppe* flew a number of missions in support of anti-partisan operations in the area. On 25 May these culminated in Operation *Rösselsprung* ('Knight's Move'), an ambitious combined air and ground assault against the headquarters of Marshal Tito's Yugoslav National Army of Liberation, which German intelligence had located high in the mountains above the small town of Drvar, some 100 kms inland from the port of Split, on the Dalmatian coast. Among the aircraft carrying the SS airborne troops of the first wave were eight Ju 87/DFS 230 combinations of II./LLG 1, plus three similarly equipped trains of 2./*Schleppgruppe* 1 (this *Schleppgruppe* was a specialised glider-towing unit, whose 2. *Staffel* had just

A night ground-attack Ju 87D of 1./NSGr 9, aircraft 'E8+CH' wears the overall scribble pattern camouflage typical of the unit

replaced their He 45 tugs with the Ju 87). Also involved in the operation were the Stukas of 13./SG 151.

Although the raid caused considerable material damage, Tito and his entourage managed to slip away. After *Rösselsprung* 2./*Schleppgruppe* 1 resumed their supply missions in the northern Balkans until being withdrawn to Germany in November. II./LLG 1, however, flew no further glider operations after the abortive attempt to capture Tito. Instead they had begun to employ their Ju 87s on purely anti-partisan sorties out of Kraljevo and Mostar. And in September 1944 their change of rôle was made official by their being redesignated *Nachtschlachtgruppe* 10.

Based at Skoplje (where 13./SG 151 had recently completed conversion on to the Fw 190), the two *Staffeln* of NSGr 10 initially flew Ju 87 night ground-attack missions

against partisans in the northern Balkans and up into Hungary, before transferring to *Luftflotte* 4 and the Eastern Front proper at year's end.

The western Allies were also faced with night harassment Ju 87s during the final 12 months of hostilities in Italy. In October 1943 ten experienced crews of NSGr 3, who had been flying Fw 58 'light twins' on the northern sector to the Russian front, had been withdrawn to Stubendorf, in Slovakia, for conversion on to the essentially similar Italian Caproni Ca 314. They were then deployed to northern Italy as 1. *Staffel* of the new NSGr 9, being joined there by 2./NSGr 9 on CR 42 biplanes shortly afterwards. As neither of these Italian types proved wholly suitable, the unit began converting to Ju 87Ds – from SG 151's not inconsiderable stocks in neighbouring Croatia – in the early spring of 1944.

Initially only 1./NSGr 9 was so re-equipped, their 'Doras' first being reported in action over the Anzio beach-head, south of Rome, late in March. Several were claimed by the anti-aircraft defences, but it was not until the night of 15/16 April that one was actually brought down within the Allied perimeter. Towards the end of May NSGr 9 reached full establishment with the arrival in Italy of the Ju 87-equipped 2./NSGr 2 from Budsslav on the central sector of the Eastern Front. This *Staffel* was subsequently redesignated to become 3./NSGr 9. And with 2./NSGr 9 now in the process of relinquishing its Fiats, the entire *Gruppe* was soon standardised on nocturnal 'Doras', complete with large flame-damper exhaust tubes and special night-flying equipment (later to include the Egon guidance system).

By now the Allies had at last broken out of the Anzio beach-head and had linked up with the main armies fighting up from the south. Through-

Another NSGr 9 Dora in a similar finish awaits the coming night's operations dispersed among the trees bordering an unidentified Italian airfield. Note the tarpaulin covering the engine, and the *Universal-Behälter*, or GP stores container – minus its nose cap – attached to the ventral bomb fork

out the remainder of the war NSGr 9 would contest their further progress as they continued to push slowly northwards towards the Alps and the Austrian border. The three *Staffeln* usually operated independently of each other, and from widely dispersed fields, attacking both the US Fifth Army's advance up the west coast, and the British 8th Army's drive up the eastern seaboard. Although each *Staffel*'s serviceable strength rarely reached double figures, the crews compensated for their lack of numbers by flying multiple missions on those nights when good visibility allowed operations to be carried out – usually around the period of the full moon.

Targets included Allied airfields, troop concentrations and assembly areas, artillery positions and road convoys. The *Gruppe* also flew sorties closer to home against the bands of Italian partisans who were becoming ever more active behind the German lines – on one memorable occasion a 'Dora' was even sent after a truck stolen from their own motor pool!

On 25 November *Gruppenkommandeur* Major Rupert Frost became the first *Nachtschlacht* pilot to be awarded the Knight's Cross. But NSGr 9's crews were suffering mounting losses. The causes would have sounded all too familiar to their desert predecessors – increased enemy opposition in the air (in NSGr 9's case mainly in the form of radar-equipped Beaufighter nightfighters), anti-aircraft ground defences and Allied bombing raids on their own bases.

By the end of 1944 – having been pushed right back up into northern Italy – the *Gruppe*'s total strength had sunk to just 12 'Doras'. In recent weeks they had been attacking enemy-occupied airfields which they themselves had vacated only a month or so before; and through which, incidentally, I./StG 1 and II./StG 2 had staged on their way to attack the *Illustrious* four years earlier.

Although their numbers rose again early in 1945, shortage of fuel was now keeping the Ju 87s grounded for much of the time. In February 1. *Staffel* began to convert to the Fw 190. No longer fully operational, 2. and 3./NSGr 9 mounted a few sporadic sorties during March and into April. But the end was at hand. On 27 April 13 airworthy 'Doras' withdrew into Austria. The lush Alpine meadows where these last of the 'Mediterranean' Stukas finally came to rest were a far cry indeed from the barren, sandy wastes of Libya.

The end of the road for the Mediterranean Stuka. One of the escapees from northern Italy – also equipped with a *Universal-Behälter* – sits half-hidden in a ramshackle barn in the Austrian Alps

APPENDICES

ORDERS OF BATTLE

BALKANS, 5 APRIL 1941

Luftwaffe

Luftflotte 4 (Vienna)

VIII. *Fliegerkorps* (Gorna Djumaja/Bulgaria)

Stab StG 2	Major Oskar Dinort	Belica-North	Ju 87B	4-4
I./StG 2	Hauptmann Hubertus Mitschhold	Belica-North	Ju 87B	30-30
			Ju 87R	9-9
III./StG 2	Hauptmann Ernst-Siegfried Steen	Belica-North	Ju 87B	38-35
I./StG 1	Major Paul-Werner Hozzel	Krainici	Ju 87R	24-23
I./StG 3	Major Walter Sigel	Belica-North	Ju 87B	30-30
			Ju 87R	9-9

Fliegerführer Graz (Austria)

Stab StG 3	Oberleutnant Karl Christ	Graz-Thalerhof	Ju 87B	3-1
II./StG 77	Hauptmann Alfons Orthofer	Graz-Thalerhof	Ju 87B	39-34

Fliegerführer Arad (Rumania)

Stab StG 77	Oberstleutnant Clemens Graf von Schönborn-Wiesentheid	Arad	Ju 87B	3-3
I./StG 77	Hauptmann Helmut Bruck	Arad	Ju 87B	39-33
III./StG 77	Major Helmuth Bode	Arad	Ju 87B	40-32

Regia Aeronautica

4a *Squadra Aerea* (Bari/Italy)

97° *Gruppo* Autonomo B.aT. Tenente Colonello Antonio Moscatelli
(209ª and 239ª *Squadriglia*) Lecce Ju 87B 20

Comando Aeronautica Albania (Tirana)

101° *Gruppo* Autonomo B.aT. Maggiore Giuseppe Donadio
(208ª and 238ª *Squadriglia*) Tirana Ju 87B 20

LUFTWAFFE STUKA PILOTS - AWARDS RECEIVED DURING MEDITERRANEAN SERVICE

KNIGHT'S CROSS WITH OAK LEAVES

Date	Name & Rank	Position/Unit	Fate
2/9/42	Sigel, Oberstleutnant Walter	GesK StG 3	KAS 8/5/44

KNIGHT'S CROSS

Date	Name & Rank	Position/Unit	Fate
14/6/41	Braun, Leutnant Rudolf	1./StG 3	S
14/6/41	Thiede, Leutnant Armin	8./StG 2	KAS 9/7/43
24/6/41	Naumann, Oberleutnant Helmut	StaKa 3./StG 3	S
5/7/41	Eppen, Oberleutnant Heinrich	StaKa 1./StG 3	KiA 4/6/42
5/7/41	Wenigmann, Oberfeldwebel Josef	2./StG 3	KiA 3/7/42
15/7/42	Kuhlmey, Hauptmann Kurt	GpK II/StG 3	S
3/9/42	Hamester, Hauptmann Bernhard	StaKa 8./StG 3	KiA 22/4/45
3/9/42	Mossdorf, Hauptmann Martin	GpK I./StG 3	PoW 11/11/42
19/9/42	Von Bargen, Oberleutnant Hans	I./StG 3	KiA 6/7/44
24/9/42	Stry, Oberleutnant Herbert	StaKa 6./StG 3	KiA 21/9/43
3/2/43	Göbel, Oberleutnant Siegfried	III./StG 3	PoW 19/3/45
18/5/43	Jähnert, Leutnant Erhard	III./StG 3	S
18/5/43[*]	Walter, Hauptmann Kurt	GpK III./StG 3	KiA 26/10/42
29/2/44[*]	Hager, Feldwebel Karl	SG 151	KAS 4/2/44
25/11/44	Frost, Major Rupert	GpK NSGr 9	S

[*] Posthumous

Abbreviations

GesK	= *Geschwaderkommodore*
GpK	= *Gruppenkommandeur*
StaKa	= *Staffelkapitän*
KiA	= Killed in action
KAS	= Killed on active service
PoW	= Prisoner of war
S	= Survived war

NB: Not included in the above list are many famous names whose decorations were undoubtedly won during the Balkan and Cretan campaigns but not awarded until *after* those involved had been transferred to the Eastern Front.

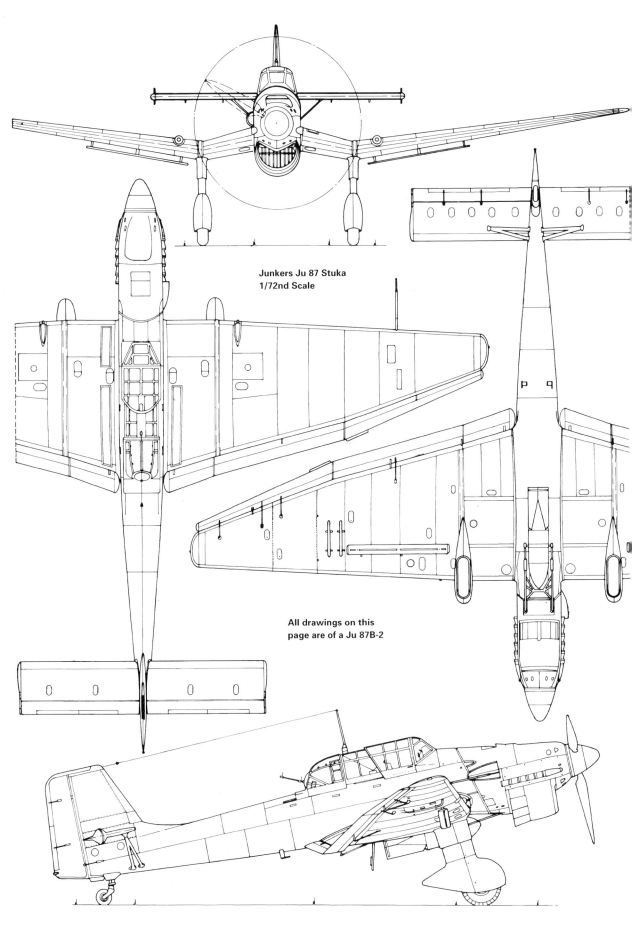

Junkers Ju 87 Stuka
1/72nd Scale

All drawings on this
page are of a Ju 87B-2

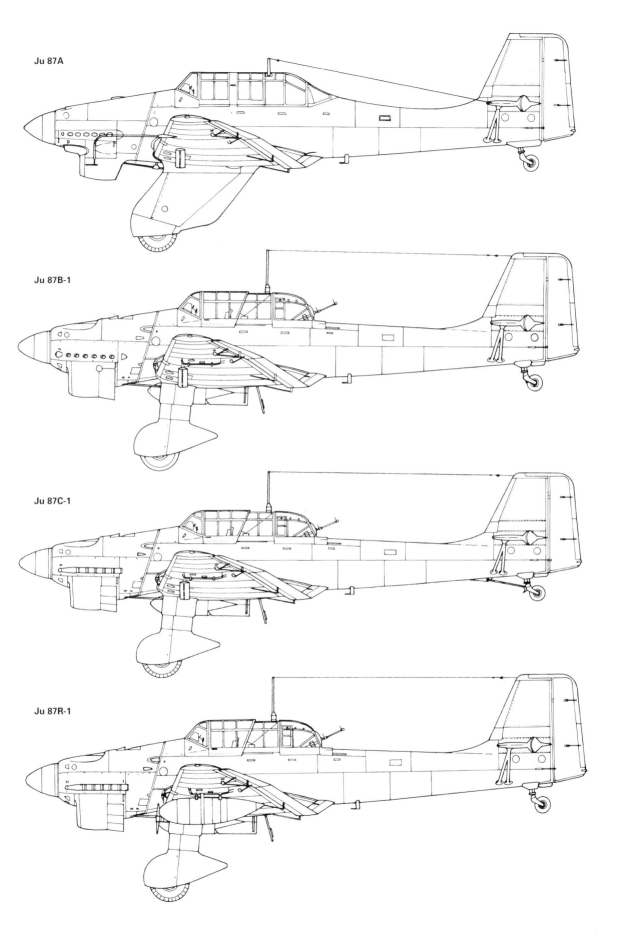

Ju 87A

Ju 87B-1

Ju 87C-1

Ju 87R-1

COLOUR PLATES

1

Ju 87R-2 'A5+HH' of 1./StG 1, Krainici/Bulgaria, April 1941

Hastily summoned from North Africa to reinforce StG 2 in Bulgaria immediately prior to the invasions of Yugoslavia and Greece, I./StG 1 nevertheless found time to apply the yellow theatre markings specified for Operation *Marita*. This particular machine is unusual, however, in having the entire tail unit (not just the rudder) painted yellow – it was presumably a formation leader's aircraft. Note the *Gruppe* emblem on the cowling – a stylised depiction of 'Hans Huckebein', a cartoon raven popular in the 19th century.

2

Ju 87R-2 'A5+JH' of 1./StG 1, Libya, February 1941

A sister-ship to 'HH' above, this aircraft also wears the standard northern European 70/71 black green/dark green finish of the early arrivals in North Africa, the only clue to the new area of operations being the white fuselage band centred behind the Balkenkreuz – white was chosen for the Luftwaffe's Mediterranean theatre markings to match those already carried by machines of the *Regia Aeronautica*. 'JH' is adorned with the figure of 'Hans Huckebein' too, although as the badge of a dive-bomber unit, he appears here to be in remarkably level flight!

3

Ju 87B-2 trop 'A5+MK' of 2./StG 1, Derna/Libya, October 1941

After their brief stint in the Balkans, I./StG 1 returned to North Africa, where they would remain until the end of the campaign (latterly as II./StG 3). The overall RLM 79 tan finish worn by 'MK' is outward evidence of the *Gruppe*'s adaptation to desert warfare. Note that the white theatre band has been relocated behind the fuselage cross, and that the otherwise omnipresent 'Hans' appears to have been granted temporary leave of absence – or perhaps he has just been inadvertently overpainted.

4

Ju 87B-2 trop. 'A5+FL' of 3./StG 1, Gambut/Libya, November 1941

This third *Staffel* machine illustrates the more common practice – initially, at least – of disrupting the overall 79 tan paintwork with a close dapple of brownish-green 80. Here, it is the white theatre marking which has disappeared (the white spinner tip is believed to indicate I.*Gruppe*) while the unit emblem is back on the cowling, albeit more difficult to make out, as too is the yellow individual aircraft letter against the background tan.

5

Ju 87R-2 'J9+AB' of II./StG 1, Comiso/Sicily,

February 1941

III./StG 1 retained the codes of its previous identity (I.(St)/TrGr 186) long after its July 1940 redesignation. Hence the anomaly here of a machine marked 'AB' indicating a III.*Gruppe Kommandeur*, for this is the aircraft usually flown by Helmut Mahlke. Note also the retention of the *Gruppe*'s 'Anchor and winged helmet' badge, but, more importantly, the yellow-painted rear section of the main undercarriage fairing and spat. This was an innovation introduced by Mahlke during the Battle of Britain to facilitate regrouping after the dive. Woe betide any pilot who ignored it, overtook the *Kommandeur* on the way home and got back to base first . . . he was on an immediate charge!

6

Ju 87R-2 'T6+AD' of the *Geschwaderstab* StG 2 'Immelmann', Belica-North/Bulgaria, April 1941

None of the four Stukas of Major Oskar Dinort's *Stabsschwarm* had the requisite Operation *Marita* yellow markings when they first arrived in Bulgaria. This was soon rectified by the unit's groundcrews, who obviously used the cowling panels as a guideline. Note the Stab emblem – the cross of the Order of Teutonic Knights.

7

Ju 87R-2 trop 'T6+HM' of 4./StG 2, Libya, circa March 1941

As the other early arrival in North Africa, II./StG 2's aircraft also initially wore the standard European 70/71 black green/dark green finish. Unlike 'A5+JH' above, this was unrelieved at first by any white theatre markings (the white spinner tip in this instance reportedly being a *Staffel*-within-*Gruppe* recognition aid). Soon after the start of their desert service 4.*Staffel* replaced their original four-leaf clover badge (see page 60 of *Osprey Combat Aircraft 2 - Junkers Ju 87 Stukageschwader 1937-41*) with the more appropriate emblem of a Luftwaffe eagle superimposed on the *Afrika Korps*' palm tree and swastika insignia. This was, however, carried on the starboard side of the cowling only (see photograph on page 42).

8

Ju 87B-2 trop 'T6+AM' of 4./StG 2, Tmimi/Libya, June 1941

Like those of I./StG 1, II./StG 2's machines also soon began to acquire (or be delivered in?) a finish of RLM 79 tan overall. But unlike the former's predilection for a dense dapple camouflage, when II./StG 2 recognised the need to break up their aircraft's outline from above, they usually opted for one of two schemes. 'AM', presumably the *Staffelkapitän*'s aircraft, provides a perfect example of the first of these – an irregular pattern comprising of large patches of brownish-green 80.

9
Ju 87B-2 trop 'T6+DM' of 4./StG 2, Gambut/Libya, October 1941

Identical in nearly all respects to the previous aircraft, 'DM' serves to illustrate that the rigours of the desert war affected machine as well as man – not just by its generally scruffy appearance, but particularly in the way the strong sunlight has quickly faded and blended the 79 and 80 tones into a far less well-defined, yet arguably more effective, camouflage scheme.

10
Ju 87B-2 'T6 +IN' of 5./StG 2, Tmimi/Libya, circa July 1941

Representative of the second type of disruptive camouflage worn by II./StG 2's aircraft is 'IN', whose tan finish has been broken up by hard-edged bands of brownish-green (although this scheme has been alternatively described as comprising areas of tan 79 applied over the basic European 70/71 paintwork). Note that this machine carries red *Staffel* trim and that, like most of those previously depicted, the individual aircraft letter is repeated on the front of both wheel spats.

11
Ju 87R-2 trop 'T6+CP' of 6./StG 2, Tmimi/Libya, July 1941

Camouflage was obviously of secondary importance when this extraordinary paint job – producing undoubtedly the most colourful of all desert Stukas – was undertaken. Such a snake motif adorned at last two different aircraft, but whether they were both flown by the same pilot – Leutnant Hubert Pölz – or were a short-lived *Staffel* (or even *Kette*) decoration is unknown. If the former, Pölz's individualism certainly stood him in good stead, for he later won the Knight's Cross and Oak Leaves on the Eastern Front, ending the war as *Kommandeur* of I./SG 151.

12
Ju 87R-2 'T6+AD' of Stab III./StG 2 'Immelmann', Belica-North/Bulgaria, April 1941

Back to Operation *Marita*, where this machine (the mount of Hauptmann Heinrich Brücker, *Gruppenkommandeur* of III./StG 2) is proof that not all aircraft in the Balkans had the yellow theatre markings. Brücker was flying 'AD' when it nosed over on landing at Krainici on 11 April 1941 – five days after the campaign had begun. Note the Patriarchal Cross emblem of III.*Gruppe*. 'Hein' Brücker (one of those whose Knight's Cross was undoubtedly won in the Mediterranean but not awarded until two days into the Russian campaign) ended the war flying the Me 262 jet.

13
Ju 87R-2 '2F+CA' of the *Geschwaderstab* StG 3, Gambut, August 1941

This tan 79/brownish-green 80 camouflaged machine bears the codes ('2F') and emblem (palm tree, mosque and minaret) adopted by the Stab of StG 3 during its early days in the desert. Its actual identity has caused some confusion in the past, for not only was the code combination '2F' allocated to various units at different times during the war, Stab StG 3 itself did not help matters by also applying it to at least three other types of aircraft they initially flew in North Africa – namely the Bf 110, Do 17 and He 111.

14
Ju 87D 'S7+AA' of the *Geschwaderstab* StG 3, Siwa Oasis, October 1942

After Karl Christ relinquished command of StG 3 to Walter Sigel, and the *Geschwader* officially incorporated the hitherto semi-autonomous I./StG 1 and II./StG 2 as its II. and III. *Gruppen* respectively, the four different unit codes in previous use ('2F', 'S1', 'A5' and 'T6'!) became one – 'S7'. Pictured here at the time of El Alamein, *Kommodore* Sigel's 'Dora' displays a standard finish, definitive markings and the Stab's blue trim.

15
Ju 87R-2 'S7+AB' of Stab I./StG 3, Tmimi/Libya, May 1942

Wearing the green trim (individual aircraft letter and halved spinner) of a *Gruppenstab* machine, this particular aircraft – Wk-Nr 6146 – is reportedly the one in which the *Gruppenkommandeur*, Knight's Cross holder Hauptmann Heinrich Eppen, was shot down by South African Tomahawks over Bir Hacheim on 4 June 1942.

16
Ju 87B-2 trop 'S7+BB' of Stab I./StG 3, Derna/Libya, circa March 1942

This otherwise perfectly standard, if albeit somewhat densely mottled, machine of I.*Gruppe*'s *Stabskette* departs from the norm by displaying a fighter-style staff chevron ahead of the fuselage code – in this instance indicating that the pilot is (presumably) the *Gruppen-Adjutant*. Although uncommon, this practice was not entirely unknown among non-fighter units. Note that the rather 'squashed' appearance of the '7' in the *Geschwader* code might suggest that this was an overpainting of I.*Gruppe*'s original 'S1'.

17
Ju 87B-2 'S1+AH' of 1./StG 3, Belica-North/Bulgaria, April 1941

The machine flown by the *Staffelkapitän* of 1./StG 3 during the Balkan campaign illustrates both the original *Gruppe* code and the fact that I./StG 3 did not carry the prescribed *Marita* yellow theatre markings either (see profile 12). In their case a narrow yellow band around the rear fuselage, extended upwards to incorporate the leading-edge of the tailfin, appears to have sufficed.

18
Ju 87B-2 trop 'S7+IH' of 1./StG 3, El Daba/Egypt,

September 1942

Eight months after I./StG 1 was officially redesignated as II./StG 3, this somewhat worse-for-wear 'Berta' still betrays clear signs of her previous identity (note the amateurish 'S7' painted over what was obviously an earlier 'A5' code). But as the 'last two' of the fuselage code appear untouched, there remains the question, did this aircraft now belong to 1./StG 3 as the fuselage markings would correctly suggest, or did it still form part of the first *Staffel* of the 'new' II.*Gruppe* – in other words, 4./StG 3?

19
Ju 87R-2 'S1+EK' of 2./StG 3, Trapani/Sicily, March 1941

No uncertainty here – a standard 70/71 European finish 2.*Staffel* machine depicted during I.*Gruppe*'s brief stay on Sicily in the spring of 1941, before transferring to Bulgaria for the Balkans campaign. Just one slight anomaly, however – although the spinner tip is in the correct *Staffel* colour red, the individual aircraft letter is outlined in white.

20
Ju 87B-2 trop 'S1+GL' of 3./StG 3, Acroma/Libya, November 1941

Back to the desert and yet more confusion. This aircraft displays a distinctive 'crazy-paving' type of camouflage pattern seen on a number of 3.*Staffel* machines, but note the emblem on the cowling! Was 3./StG 3 given some ex-I./StG 1 machines to make good its losses – or did the latter unit also wear the 'S1' fuselage code in the months immediately prior to its redesignation?

21
Ju 87B-2 trop 'S7+HL' of 3./StG 3, El Daba/Egypt, September 1942

On slightly safer ground with this aircraft of 3.*Staffel*, although even here there appear definite signs of overpainting behind the current 'last two'. Note that the position of the white theatre band ahead of the fuselage Balkenkreuz was unusual, but not unique.

22
Ju 87D 'S7+CL' of 3./StG 3, Gambut/Libya, November 1942

Proving that I./StG 3 finally got their markings act together, this perfectly standard tan 79 'Dora' is pictured in the immediate aftermath of El Alamein, and shortly before the *Gruppe* was withdrawn for rest and refit. Note the yellow spinner tip and a name (*Inge?*) in small white letters on the engine cowling.

23
Ju 87R-2 'S7+EM' of 4./StG 3, Tmimi/Libya, May 1942

Looking definitely 'war-weary', this tan 79/brownish-green 80 aircraft of 4.*Staffel* is pictured shortly before II.*Gruppe* re-equipped with Ju 87Ds. Note that the individual aircraft letter 'E' is repeated on the white

underwing tips, and that the machine is carrying a cluster of fragmentation bombs in place of underwing tanks.

24
Ju 87R-2 'S7+DN' of 5./StG 3, Derna/Libya, March 1942

Pictured only weeks earlier than the machine in the previous profile, this densely-dappled 5.*Staffel* aircraft is showing equal signs of wear and tear. More unusual are the location and the extremely narrow width of the white theatre band around the aft fuselage, and the obviously hand-painted and rather cramped '7' – is the latter another indication that some machines of I./StG 1 did indeed carry the 'S1' code before being redesignated II./StG 3?

25
Ju 87D 'S7+EP' of 6./StG 3, El Aouina/Tunisia, December 1942

Representative of the aircraft flown by II.*Gruppe* at the start of the Tunisian campaign, 'EP' has reverted to European-style 70/71 finish, plus white theatre band. Note that the underwing 'M' is not part of the unit code, but the last letter of the machine's original *Stammkennzeichen* (the Ju 87, more than any other operational type, often retained this four-part basic identity code across the undersurface of the wings). Nice to see, too, that the units past history hasn't been forgotten – look who's back on the cowling!

26
Ju 87D 'S7+KR' of 7./StG 3, Libya, circa December 1942

III.*Gruppe* also flew singularly inappropriate dark green/black green 'Doras' during their final retreat across Libya (presumably there was no time for such niceties as local camouflage). Modellers should note, however, that many machines of 7./StG 3 carried both their individual aircraft letter *and* the *Staffel* designator (in this case 'KR') in white on the starboard side of the fuselage (to the right of the Balkenkreuz).

27
Ju 87B-2 'S2+AB' of Stab I./StG 77, Argos/Greece, May 1941

Still resplendent in their Operation *Marita* yellow livery, aircraft of I./StG 77, including that of the *Gruppenkommandeur* Hauptmann Helmut Bruck pictured here, moved from Yugoslavia down into southern Greece to carry out operations against Crete. Note the *Gruppenstab* badge – a wolf's head – on the standardised background shield used by all units of StG 77. Bruck himself rose to the rank of Oberst, and commanded SG 151 during the final weeks of the war.

28
Ju 87B-2 'S2+AP' of 6./StG 77, Graz/Austria, April 1941

A symphony in yellow – yellow theatre markings, yellow *Staffel* letter and trim – this 6.*Staffel* machine is part of II./StG 77, which attacked Yugoslavia from the north, before likewise moving down to Argos to participate in the Cretan campaign. Note here too the *Staffel* badge (a charging black bull) on the same style of shield as above, but with the upper indented field in red to indicate II.*Gruppe*.

29

Ju 87D 'D3+GK' of 2./NSGr 2, northern Italy, circa June 1944

In stark contrast to the colourful machine above, this 'Dora' depicts the sombre finish in which 2./NSGr 2's aircraft first arrived from the Eastern Front to begin operations in Italy (where they were later redesignated 3./NSGr 9). Note that, in addition to the fuselage markings, the machine also carries an individual number on the rudder. This was a common practice among Eastern Front *Nachtschlachtgruppen*, but was discontinued by 2.*Staffel* shortly after its transfer to the Mediterranean.

30

Ju 87D 'E8+NH' of 1./NSGr 9, Bologna/Italy, May 1944

Whereas 2./NSGr 2's machines flew in from Russia, 1./NSGr 9's first Ju 87s came from nearer to hand, including, it is believed, from SG 151 in neighbouring Croatia. Like 'GK' above, this early 1.*Staffel* aircraft is also equipped with exhaust flame damper tubes and muzzle flash eliminators, but the retention of a white theatre band seems a little inappropriate for nocturnal operations.

31

Ju 87D 'E8+LK' of 2./NSGr 9, Ghedi/Italy, September 1944

All aircraft of NSGr 9 were soon reduced to a standard anonymity by the application of a close meander pattern overall. This was either in tan brown (as here on 'LK') or blue-grey, and was usually used to tone down the national insignia as well – note that on this machine the underwing crosses have been completely overpainted. Note too that even at this late stage of the war Dinort's extended fuse rods are still in use.

32

Ju 87R 'H4+MM' of 4./LLG 1, Aix les Milles/southern France, July 1943

An aircraft in standard 70/71 black green/dark green camouflage with white theatre band and *Staffel* markings – nothing out of the ordinary, except for that small attachment just behind the tailwheel, which is the only indication that 'MM' is, in fact, a glider-tug.

33

Ju 87B-2 'SH+SV' of *Stukaschule* 2, Foggia/Italy, circa Summer 1942

Also sporting a white Mediterranean theatre band, this machine advertises its function much more clearly. The large white numerals on the wheelspat can only mean that it belongs to a training establishment – specifically to *Stukaschule* 2, which vacated Graz-Thalerhof for Italy in December 1941.

34

Ju 87B-2 of 237a *Squadriglia*, 96° *Gruppo*, Lecce-Galatina/Italy, Autumn 1940

It was at Graz-Thalerhof (see above) that the first of the *Regia Aeronautica* Ju 87 pilots were trained before returning to Italy to begin operations as the 96° *Gruppo*. Their fist aircraft were ex-Luftwaffe machines, such as that depicted here, with the German national insignia overpainted and replaced by a large white tail cross. As yet there appear to be no unit markings – except for the cartoon on the fuselage showing a red devil aiming a bomb . . . the original *Picchiatello* perhaps?

35

Ju 87R-2 of 239a *Squadriglia*, 97° *Gruppo*, Lecce-Galatina/Italy, April 1941

The second Italian Ju 87 *Gruppo*, 97°, also initially flew ex-Luftwaffe Stukas – note the overpainted insignia again. They took over from 96° at Lecce, which remained their base throughout the Balkan campaign. In contrast to that above, this machine sports a wealth of markings – a yellow campaign nose-band, underwing *fasces*, a unit badge on the spat (consisting of a duck fitted with a ring-and-bead sight and carrying a full bomb load – between its feet and underwing! – diving on an enemy ship), the *squadriglia* number on a white theatre band, an abbreviated tail cross and what appear to be ship silhouettes below the Wk-Nr (7065) on the tailfin!

36

Ju 87R-2 of 208a *Squadriglia*, 101° *Gruppo*, Trapani/Sicily, Spring 1941

101° *Gruppo* fought the Balkan campaign from Tirana, in Albania, after which it was transferred to Sicily for operations against Malta. Representative of the unit's aircraft at this time, the overpainting of the recent Balkan yellow nose-band is clearly evident on this 208a *Squadriglia* machine. Note also that the *squadriglia* number is painted in white ahead of the Mediterranean theatre band, rather than being superimposed on it in black.

37

Ju 87D of 207a *Squadriglia*, 103° *Gruppo*, Sardinia, Summer 1943

Belonging to one of the two *gruppi* to be equipped with the Ju 87D, this machine of 207a *Squadriglia* is depicted during the unit's working-up period on Sardinia. Note that this *squadriglia* carries its number in large numerals on a wide theatre band and that, for the first time, an individual aircraft number – 'Red 12' – is also shown. Note also the spinner tip in the *squadriglia* colour, Luftwaffe style, and the absence of wheel fairings. It is reported that 103° *Gruppo* was wiped out during the Sicilian campaign.

38
Ju 87D of 216a *Squadriglia,* 121° *Gruppo,* Sardinia, September 1943

Unlike 103° *Gruppo,* a handful of machines of the other Ju 87D-equipped gruppo, 121°, survived the fighting in Sicily and returned to Sardinia. This 216ᵃ *Squadriglia* aircraft illustrates the unit's rather unusual markings: a white squadriglia designator ahead of the fuselage band, with what is presumably an individual aircraft number depicted in what appear to be Roman numerals on the band itself.

39.
Ju 87D of the *Nucleo Volo Stormo Trasporti,* Lecce/Italy, circa Summer 1944

After the Italian surrender, two of the five surviving 'Doras' of 121° *Gruppo* served with the Italian Co-Belligerent Air Force as target-towing tugs for the training of Allied bomber crew air gunners (note the target tow-hook attachment behind the tailwheel). Apart from new Italian roundels, markings were restricted to the small NVST initials and aircraft number '1' in white on the tailfin, and the even smaller military serial MM100410 on the lower fuselage.

Figure Plates

1

Oberleutnant Hartmut Schairer, *Staffelkapitän* of 7./StG 1 at Comiso, on Sicily, in February 1941. Newly-arrived in the Mediterranean theatre from northern France, Schairer wears standard Luftwaffe early-war multi-zippered flying suit with officer's field cap (officially called a *Fliegermütze,* but more colloquially known as the '*Schiffchen*' – 'Little Ship'). Note also the cloth patch, carried on both sleeves, denoting rank. Schairer claimed the sinking of one destroyer and four merchantmen, plus damage to another six, during his brief period of service in the Mediterranean. He was killed on 19 July 1942 after transfer to the Eastern Front.

2

Maggiore Giuseppe Donadio, *Comandante* of 101° *Gruppo* B.aT. at Tirana, in Albania, in April 1941. He is depicted here wearing typical Italian flying garb of the period, combining a brownish-olive zippered flight-blouse (with fur collar and elasticated cuffs and waist band) with baggy flight trousers in RA blue. Note the latter's thigh patch pockets, more rectangular and less deep than the Luftwaffe pattern. Note, too, the Italian officer's peaked cap and badges of rank worn at the cuff.

3

Hauptmann Helmut Mahlke, *Gruppenkommandeur* of III./StG 1, Derna/Libya, April 1941. Schairer's CO illustrates the makeshift nature of the dress code adopted when two of III./StG 1's *Staffeln* were suddenly despatched to North Africa. From the waist up

Helmut Mahlke is archetypal early *Afrika Korps* – lightweight tan tunic, solar topee and sand goggles. Only the pilot's badge below the Iron Cross on his left breast, and the gold-yellow piping on his shoulder tabs, indicate his true branch of service – as, of course, do the breeches and those highly unsuitable boots! Mahlke survived to rejoin the postwar *Bundesluftwaffe,* retiring with the rank of Generalleutnant in 1970.

4

Major Walter Enneccerus, *Gruppenkommandeur* of II./StG 2 at Tmimi, in Libya, during the summer of 1941. Completely 'tropicalised' from head to foot, the legendary 'Ennec' shows what the well-dressed pilot was wearing at the height of the desert campaign – officer's peaked cap with white cloth cover, short-sleeved shirt, officer's leather belt with holstered pistol, shorts, ankle-socks and sandals. Note the Knight's Cross at his throat, the triangular cloth Luftwaffe eagle patch on the right breast and the dive-bomber's clasp on the left. After nearly two years in North Africa, Enneccerus served the remainder of the war in a succession of senior staff positions. He died in Germany in 1971.

5

Oberstleutnant Walter Sigel, *Geschwaderkommodore* of StG 3 at Siwa Oasis, in Egypt, in September 1942. Wearing the same pattern shirt as Enneccerus, Sigel rings the changes with his trappings, including Oberstleutnant's shoulder tabs, Knight's Cross with newly-awarded Oak Leaves at his throat, Iron Cross on the left pocket and German Cross on the right. Belt and holster are also the same, but the rest of Sigel's outfit is late tropical issue – special long-peaked cap (with goggles), tan single-pocket flight trousers and thick-soled lace-up boots. Best remembered as a desert campaigner, Sigel's last resting place could not be further removed from the heat and dust of North Africa. Promoted to the office of *Fliegerführer* in Norway, he was killed during an inspection flight on 8 May 1944 when his Fieseler *Storch* crashed after hitting power-lines stretched across Trondheim Fjord.

6

Oberleutnant Herbert Stry, *Staffelkapitän* of 5./StG 3 at Martuba, in Libya, in April 1942. A long-serving member of II./StG 2, Stry was one of the pilots who damaged the carrier HMS *Illustrious* whilst sheltering in Maltese docks in January 1941. Pictured here shortly after becoming *Staffelkapitän* of 5./StG 3, he too favours tropical flight trousers and desert boots. He pairs them with a lightweight tunic, whose shoulder tabs are all but hidden by the early-pattern kapok life-jacket – an essential item during the many over-water sorties flown during the North African campaign. Later posted to take over 6.*Staffel,* Stry was killed by the premature explosion of his own bomb while attacking Italian positions at Davgata, on the island of Cephalonia, on 21 September 1943.